"I have known Elaine for many y[...] [...]
to God, to prayer, and to God's people. This book expresses her
ongoing commitment to pray earnestly, clearly, and forcefully. It
should be read by every Christian, especially by Christian leaders."

—DR. HENRY BLACKABY, author of *Experiencing God*

"God bless Elaine Helms for calling the church to prayer. It is
imperative that we understand with great clarity the power, the
principles, and the privilege of prayer."

—BABBIE MASON, award-winning singer, songwriter,

and Bible study teacher

"Elaine Helms brilliantly elicits a response of quietness, confidence,
and humility before our heavenly Father. Calling us to acknowledge our dependency *upon* God and actively to pursue our delight
in God, her book awakens longings for intimacy with the Father;
guides us to identify and deal with sinful, idolatrous preoccupa-
tions that distract us from that intimacy; and urges us to embrace
God's gracious invitation to experience covenant relationship with
Him."

—DR. ROGER S. "SING" OLDHAM, vice president for Convention

communications and relations, Executive Committee of the

Southern Baptist Convention

"Elaine Helms has become a significant prayer leader who God has used in the lives of many followers of Jesus in recent years. I am grateful that she is sharing many of the insights on prayer that the Lord has taught her over the years. I highly recommend this wonderful book to you."

—DR. PAUL CEDAR, chairman, CEO, Mission America Coalition

"God takes His rightful position front and center in Elaine Helm's new book, *Prayer Without Limits*. The powerful message of this book is that we as believers are privileged to work with God through the means of prayer. Prayer is not so much trying to get things from God, as it is partnering with God in accomplishing His purposes."

—DAVE BUTTS, chairman, America's National Prayer Committee

"Elaine Helms has done it again. In her clear and direct style, she has pointed the reader to a more effective prayer life. The book's stated purpose—to help us become people that God can trust with His purposes and that will attribute the glory back to Him—saturates the book and serves as a challenge for the reader to advance from *Prayer 101* to *Prayer Without Limits*."

—DR. DAN R. CRAWFORD, senior professor of evangelism and missions; chair of prayer, emeritus, at Southwestern Baptist Theological Seminary

"This book is a breath of fresh air, for it demonstrates that knee exercise activates the weapons of spiritual warfare, devastating an already defeated foe. When Elaine Helms speaks on prayer, our team listens. She encourages the reader to tap into the intimate victory in Christ through prayer. Elaine shares how God's sovereign work in and through prayer overcomes obstacles so we can depend solely on the Lord. As I read, I was convicted to exercise believing prayer and to 'put feet' to prayer by being bold. I highly recommend *Prayer Without Limits*."

—DR. TOM PHILLIPS, vice president, The Billy Graham Library

"As Americans we want to win; we want our teams to win, we want to win at work . . . we are driven people. Elaine Helms in *Prayer Without Limits* shows us not only where real victory lies, in a truly effective one-on-one prayer relationship with God the Father, but she guides us through the pitfalls to which so many of us succumb, frustrating our prayer lives. *Prayer Without Limits* is a game-plan for true victory, maturity, and a satisfying, God-glorifying life of prayer."

—JOHN GLENN FARISH, managing director, Russell Reynolds Associates

"Elaine Helms writes out of her experience as a seasoned prayer leader and one who recognizes the urgency of our day. She eagerly invites the church to engage fully in praying 'audacious, seemingly impossible prayers.' Her longing is for fellow believers to be empowered and emboldened to stand up for our King and pray to the honor of His name. It's a calling for every believer, and Elaine's practical guide will take any willing follower of Christ on a bold journey of praying God's purposes. Thank you, Elaine. May another great awakening be the answer to our prayers!"

—CAROL MADISON, editor, *Prayer Connect* magazine

"Elaine Helms has written a book that explains in practical terms how we can have conversations with God that impact our lives and our loved ones—and the world. She shares insight on the obstacles to prayer and how to overcome them, reminding us of the weapons God provides to help us win spiritual battles. Elaine's *Prayer Without Limits* can help one develop a prayer life that gives joy others will notice and open doors to share the love of Jesus, so that many will come to know Him as Savior."

—REV. BRYANT WRIGHT, senior pastor,
Johnson Ferry Baptist Church of Marietta, Georgia

"I've known Elaine almost 25 years, have seen her walk with God, her integrity, and how her relationship with Him has increasingly deepened over the years. The value of a book on prayer comes from the degree of value of the author's prayer life, and for this reason

I recommend *Prayer Without Limits.* As far as the book itself goes, I find something about the framework of her book unique from most books on prayer that you will find most beneficial. She describes how a person's prayer life changes as his or her relationship with God deepens over time. Just as a son or daughter relates to an earthly father differently in preschool, elementary, teenage, and adult stages, so our prayer life changes as we mature. This book gives you a handle on where God is taking you and how you will change on the journey."

—DR. JOHN FRANKLIN, president, John Franklin Ministries

"Biblical, insightful, and practical. Elaine writes as if she is speaking directly to the reader. *Prayer Without Limits* is prayer, rooted in the lifelong journey of discipleship. Talking with God, filled with and yielded to the Holy Spirit, brings glory to our Father in heaven. *Prayer Without Limits* gives a good way to journey toward passionate dependence upon God; it begins and ends with God.

—REV. PHIL MIGLIORATTI, founder of National Pastors' Prayer Network; community manager, Pray! Network

"As I read *Prayer Without Limits* the primary theme that seemed to surface was maturity. Elaine challenges readers to grow up, to press toward the 'higher ground' of personal holiness that will allow the pray-er to become a fit vessel for the Spirit's intercessory work."

"Prayer is the most powerful weapon available to the believer who wants to have an impact for the sake of the kingdom. In her new book *Prayer Without Limits*, Elaine Helms reminds us that maturing in prayer is accepting God's invitation to engage in the spiritual battle for the souls of the lost around the world. If you are hungering to grow in your prayer life, I encourage you to read this book."

"This book reminded, challenged, and encouraged me to passionately pursue energetic, enthusiastic, extraordinary, purposeful prayer as a way of life so that the power of God can abide in my person, practicum, and polity! For dialoguing with the divine and Spirit-led fasting are the foundation for the manifestation of His glory through spiritual awakening, which will bring repentance for the sinner and revival for the saints. Every blood-bought, born-again believer in the body of Christ *must read* and *meditate* on this charge to be an *intercessor, unified* with other believers by His Spirit!

Our battle is not against flesh and blood but against principalities and powers, spiritual wickedness in high places (Ephesians 6:12)! I say thank You, Lord, for depositing this *rhema* word into Elaine Helms, to help equip us to get serious about fighting the battle where the battle is, in the heavenlies (v. 18). May the Lord bless you, Elaine, for allowing Him to use you to give this blessing that will revolutionize relationships with the Redeemer, fix fractures in the fellowship, and enlarge the remnant for authentic kingdom living!"

—REV. K. MARSHALL WILLIAMS SR., pastor, Nazarene Baptist Church of Philadelphia, Pennsylvania; president National African American Fellowship, Southern Baptist Convention

"Elaine Helm's passion for prayer is unmistakable. Her gentle grace evidences personal time with the Lord.

Prayer Without Limits is her latest book. It is written simply; it is understandable—as a book on prayer should be. It is the ideological progression that makes the book unique. Elaine begins with a focus on the sovereignty of God—that is where prayer must begin, not with us, but with Him. Not with technique, but with a healthy theology of God and prayer. She then pinpoints, in a plain but gracious manner, the serious issues in all our lives that prevent victory and effective ministry. The next steps move the reader to growth in prayer, then onward toward maturity in prayer, and then to that place in Christ to which every sincere believer aspires—an alignment by which Christ works in us and through us, where He is glorified and our lives are measurably impactful.

Each chapter contains a prayer, and points for reflection. Elaine has given us more than a book. She has given us a plan for growth in our relationship with God, in Christ, by prayer. A plan to become animated, involved Christians fulfilling our obligation to the Great Commission with joy."

—P. DOUGLAS SMALL, coordinator for prayer ministries,
Church of God of Cleveland, Tennessee

"A slogan I live by is, 'The work of God is done on our knees. Then we go find out what happened.' Elaine Helms believes that, too, and she has provided profound and practical help for living it out. *Prayer Without Limits* is a challenge, an inspiration, and a guide to a truer walk with Jesus and greater effectiveness in praying."

—MRS. STEVE (JUDY) DOUGLASS, Office of the President,
women's resources, Campus Crusade for Christ/Cru; writer, speaker,
encourager; founder, Prayer for Prodigals

"In my nearly 40 years of ministry, I have encountered some very special people whose names become synonymous with prayer; Elaine Helms is just such a person! Elaine's dedication and commitment to the spiritual discipline of prayer are well-known. To be on her prayer list is a blessing, because you *know* she will prevail in prayer for you. Elaine, in *Prayer Without Limits*, shares what she has gleaned from the Scriptures as it relates to prayer. She shares with depth, wisdom, and practicality how to prepare for victory, rather than just vaguely hope that somehow God will come through. Elaine is a mighty woman of prayer, and she can help you to lay hold of heaven in becoming the person of prayer you've always desired to be!"

—DR. DWIGHT "IKE" REIGHARD, president/CEO MUST Ministries; senior pastor, Piedmont Church of Marietta, Georgia

"I strongly recommend this book to experience — for revival through prayer — with the biblical insights to begin in our churches first and to spread across our land. It is about victorious Christian living through practical prayer life, trusting in Christ."

—DR. PAUL KIM, pastor emeritus, Antioch Baptist Church of Cambridge, Massachusetts

"In *Prayer Without Limits,* the author, Elaine Helms, provides the church a biblically based practical tool on prayer. The purpose of this book is to help us become a cleansed people that God can trust with His purposes, who bring glory to His name, and encourage and equip the church to carry out His mission. I have no doubt that this resource will move us toward a deeper and enriched prayer life. I commend it to you."

—DR. BOBBY S. SENA, Hispanic relations consultant, the Executive Committee of the Southern Baptist Convention

"This is not your ordinary book on prayer! Elaine Helms manages to bring together not only wonderful and strong encouragements to prayer, but she also graciously deals with many of the issues that are so often used by the enemy to keep a person's prayer life in a diminished place. It is the kind of book the church needs. The truths set forth in this book have been written down after much time in the laboratory of the prayer room. The reader will find that they are within reach of any heart that longs for the Lord to 'teach us to pray.' I believe that God will use this book to issue a fresh, strong, and clear call to His people to 'continue in prayer and watch in the same with thanksgiving.' I highly recommend a prayerful reading and heeding of this book."

—DR. AL WHITTINGHILL, Ambassadors for Christ International

PRAYER

WITHOUT LIMITS

OTHER NEW HOPE® BOOKS

by Elaine Helms

Prayer 101: What Every Intercessor Needs to Know

PRAYER
WITHOUT LIMITS

EXPANDING YOUR RELATIONSHIP WITH GOD

ELAINE HELMS

NEW HOPE®
PUBLISHERS
Gospel-Centered. Missions-Driven.

BIRMINGHAM, ALABAMA

New Hope® Publishers
P. O. Box 12065
Birmingham, AL 35202-2065
NewHopeDigital.com
New Hope Publishers is a division of WMU®.

Library of Congress Control Number: 2014957542

All Scripture quotations, unless otherwise indicated, are taken from the New American Standard Bible®, Copyright © 1960, 1962, 1963, 1968, 1971, 1972, 1973, 1975, 1977, 1995 by The Lockman Foundation Used by permission.
Scripture quotations marked (KJV) are taken from The Holy Bible, King James Version.

Cover Designer: Kay Bishop
Interior Designer: Glynese Northam

ISBN-10: 1-59669-428-9
ISBN-13: 978-1-59669-428-6
N154107 · 0415 · 2M1

Dedication

Father,

I dedicate this book to You, praying this will bring You glory. It is about how great You are and the victory You want us to have over the world. Thank You for working through Your people. Keep us clean, consecrated, and committed to You and Your purposes. Every good thing and every perfect gift is from above, so anything good in this book is from You. I submit it back to You for the cleansing, preparation, and equipping of the saints for the work of victorious prayer.

May this be a tool You can use to awaken Your people — Your bride — the church, to pray the promises You have given us into fruition, to pray the prayers You want prayed, and to give You no rest until Your work of reviving and restoring Your people is accomplished. Help us, Lord, to fall more in love with You, and to make disciples who will make disciples who also love You whole-heartedly. I pray that our prayers for Your kingdom to come and Your will to be done on earth as it is in heaven are more fully realized through this book. May the readers of this book be drawn into a deep loving relationship with You, dear Father.

In Jesus' name, amen.

In honor of the remnant that is willing to linger with our Father in prayer, to prepare the bride of Christ for our Bridegroom.

Epigraph

"But thanks be to God, who gives us the victory through our Lord Jesus Christ"

(1 CORINTHIANS 15:57).

"Prayer warriors are the most frightening, powerful, demon-chasing, world-moving beings on earth. . . . Prayer warriors are positioned by God to stand in faith for their families and churches and cities. Prayer is stronger than kings and mightier than armies. Prayer is the most powerful force on earth."

—FRANCIS FRANGIPANE

Contents

Acknowledgments

I thank God for my husband, Joel, for being such an encouraging, faithful reader, and for our children, Julie, Shannon, and Joel Jr., for being the cheering squad with influential and thought-provoking comments. Thanks to Joel Jr. for sharing an answered prayer story to include. It was humbling to write on this topic because God kept bringing me under conviction. I am most thankful to God for not giving up on my consecration process.

I give sincere thanks to the many prayer supporters, especially Tracy Atcheson, who mobilized them to pray. Thanks to all in our small group who prayed and to those who studied the material to refine it; with special thanks to Virginia Wiggins, Don and Nancy Waldroup, Julio and Glenda Espana, Ed and Suzanne Weiss, Ty and Dee Gregory, John and Julia Jefferson, Terry and Linda Martin, and Shirley Morgan for sharing their perspectives.

My appreciation goes to you as you read and study this book. May God use it to draw you closer to Him and into the praying remnant that will not give up.

Introduction

"Pray, then, in this way: 'Our Father who is in heaven, hallowed be Your name. Your kingdom come. Your will be done, on earth as it is in heaven.'"

(MATTHEW 6:9–10).

The early church turned their "world upside down" (Acts 17:6 KJV). We want present-day Christians to do the same. Instead, we may be tiptoeing by prayer rather than plunging into the power and connection God from the beginning intended for prayer to be in His followers' lives. In Romans 13:11, Paul says we need to wake up, "It is already the hour for you to awaken from sleep."

God created us in His own image so that we could have fellowship with Him and participate in His work (Genesis 1:26–28). God's ultimate desire is repeated throughout His Word. In 2 Corinthians 6:16 Paul alludes to several Old Testament passages in Exodus 29:45; Leviticus 26:12; Jeremiah

31:1; and Ezekiel 37:27, among others where God says, "I will dwell in them and walk among them; and I will be their God and they shall be My people."

When we understand the significance of spending time in prayer — both listening and talking with God — prayer takes on a deeper, more stimulating dimension. Prayer is not ordinary but extraordinary. God is the One who loves us, who is in control, and who is calling us to join Him in His work. How can we sleep at a time like this?

From the very beginning, God has interacted and communicated with people He created. In the cool of the day, He walked and talked with Adam in the Garden of Eden and gave him meaningful work to do before the fall. Examples are in Genesis 2:15, cultivating and keeping the garden; and in 2:19, naming the animals. God gave Noah clear directions for building an ark in Genesis 6:13–22. Noah listened, understood, and obeyed. God spoke with Abraham in Genesis 22:1–2 to tell him to sacrifice his son as a test of his faith. He continually spoke to Abraham, Isaac, Jacob, Moses, Joshua, the judges, and the prophets.

Jesus came as the incarnate Word of God (John 1:14) and communicated with humanity in-person. Then the ultimate expression of God's desire to know us intimately was the giving of His Holy Spirit to dwell in us. We really can "pray without ceasing" as commanded in 1 Thessalonians 5:17.

When the disciples asked Jesus to teach them to pray, He gave them a pattern for prayer, which is recorded for us in

Matthew 6:9–13 and Luke 11:2–4. They observed that Jesus talked often with His Father and was directed and empowered by those times; they wanted to pray like Him. The pattern Jesus gave could be summed up: "[Cast] all your anxiety upon Him, because He cares for you" (1 Peter 5:7).

When we believe and trust God for our provision, forgiveness, and protection (see Matthew 6:25–33), then we can spend the bulk of our prayertimes focused on God. There is more time for seeking His kingdom on earth as it is in heaven and for His will to be done in our lives and in the world around us. That involves fewer words from us and a lot more listening to Him.

Jesus said, "Seek first [God's] kingdom and His righteousness, and all these things will be added to you" (Matthew 6:33). When we focus on Him and His purposes, the temporary things that can so consume our prayers are taken care of by our great Provider, Healer, and Protector.

Our prayers on earth truly do affect what is happening with the principalities and powers at work in the world because of the Fall of man. Paul explains in Ephesians, "For our struggle is not against flesh and blood, but against the rulers, against the powers, against the world forces of this darkness, against the spiritual forces of wickedness in the heavenly places" (Ephesians 6:12).

We are given just the right uniform, the armor of God, for our assignment. "With all prayer and petition pray *at all times* in the Spirit, and with this in view, be on the alert with all perseverance and petition for all the saints"(v. 18, author's emphasis). Our work is to believe; our assignment is to pray.

This endurance in prayer is not child's play nor for the faint of heart, but we can have confidence because God initiates our prayers, empowers us to pray, and then answers our prayers. God says, "For as the heavens are higher than the earth, so are My ways higher than your ways, and My thoughts than your thoughts" (Isaiah 55:9). We will pray well when we learn to listen to the One with the wisdom and the plan for eternity (see Jeremiah 33:3).

Would you like for us as Christians today to be like the early church, which turned the world upside down? We want our world to notice, marveling that we have been with Jesus, as they did in Acts 4:13. God says in Malachi 3:6, "For I, the LORD, do not change." Society, however, with "every man [doing] what [is] right in his own eyes" (Judges 17:6) is continually decadent. It has little semblance to God's kingdom "on earth as it is in heaven" (Matthew 6:10).

We can make a difference, though, and that is why I am writing. We can make a difference by praying according to God's heart. The battle for the soul of the church will be won on our knees. God reminds us that it is "'not by might, nor by power, but by My Spirit,' says the LORD of hosts" (Zechariah 4:6).

There is often a gap between God's plan, and His power "to do exceeding abundantly above all that we ask or think" (Ephesians 3:20 KJV) and what we may see happening in the church in the world today. God is looking for a mature church with mature intercessors He can trust to pray what He directs (read more about maturity in chapter 4). When Jesus, the Bridegroom, comes again for His bride, the church, He will be looking for a mature bride. Christians cannot remain as newborns only able to handle milk (Hebrews 5:13).

The way to go deeper with God is to get to know Him and understand His character. So in this book, we will examine the greatness of God and how He has shown Himself in control throughout Scripture. We will scrutinize some of the obstacles we bring to prayer and also address actions we can take to obtain the effectiveness God intends for us to employ in prayer, through the power of the Holy Spirit unleashed in our lives.

We can grow into spiritual maturity through a better understanding of prayer as preparation for reigning with Jesus in eternity (see 2 Timothy 2:12; Revelation 3:21; 20:6). God is looking for those who will not only talk and theorize about prayer but also pray continually for eternal purposes.

Before eternity, though, God has work for us to do here on earth (Ephesians 2:10). God desires for none to perish and calls us to be His fellow workers toward that end. To give you more of an idea of what to expect, here are chapter highlights.

CHAPTER 1 addresses the sovereignty of God and His all-powerful ability. In order to mature in Christ and become a fellow worker that God can trust with His eternal purposes, we need to better understand His character. Highlighting the reality of God's redemptive power and continual intimacy with His people throughout Scripture gives us a clearer perspective. The God we address in prayer exceeds all our expectations and wants us to know Him as intimately today.

CHAPTER 2 is an evaluation of some of the obstacles we unintentionally bring to prayer and how they can quench the Holy Spirit's power that could be working in us. There may be a blind spot or a comfortable sin we have overlooked. Idolatry in the twenty-first century and influences of the world around us aid our subtle slide into toleration of sin. Rather than basing acceptable behavior and attitudes on the world or even church tradition, we look to Scripture for God's standard of measure and for His cleansing.

CHAPTER 3 focuses on actions we can take and good habits we can form to unleash the power of the Holy Spirit to work through our prayers. We cover ways to effectively live a lifestyle of prayer so that we can truly pray without ceasing, be consecrated to God for His use, and grow into God-pleasing, believing prayer intercessors. Scripture demonstrates the connection between our obedience and remembering the mighty acts of God so we can be alert and stay in right standing with God.

CHAPTER 4 discusses the importance of maturing in our walk with God so our prayers will accomplish His purposes and bring Him glory. Those who endure to the end will be invited to sit with Jesus on His throne in heaven to reign with Him. This chapter covers five steps to maturity that prepare us for eternity with Jesus as well as for the possibly turbulent road ahead of us in the meantime.

CHAPTER 5 challenges us to work with God in prayer, for Jesus calls us His fellow workers. Knowing that God desires for none to perish, we discover the importance of supporting fellow believers by praying for their boldness as well as praying for those who do not yet know Jesus as Savior.

We must be ready to be answers to our own prayers, to clearly share our reason for the hope within us (1 Peter 3:15). We can do so by being tuned into the One with whom we speak in prayer, that we will naturally be fellow workers with Christ in His work of redeeming a lost world. Working with God begins with Spirit-led and empowered prayer.

We may be doing lots of praying, but if there is no clear passion for and dependence on God in our lives, churches, and society—something is wrong. The reason I write is to help us become a pure people God can trust with His purposes and who will attribute the glory to Him. It is my prayer that this book will be a tool God can use to encourage and equip us for what He is calling us to be and do. In Acts 17:11, Luke tells us about the early Christians in Berea: "Now these were more noble-minded than those in Thessalonica, for they received the word with great eagerness, examining the Scriptures daily, to see whether these things were so." We will lean heavily on His Word to learn His ways, so I encourage you to keep your Bible handy as you read, so you can, like the Bereans, see "whether these things [are] so."

May the Holy Spirit reveal God's truth to you and give clear direction for your journey into a victorious prayer life that far exceeds your expectations.

CHAPTER ONE

GOD HAS ALL-POWERFUL ABILITY

"Give me one hundred preachers who fear nothing but sin and desire nothing but God, and I care not a straw whether they be clergymen or laymen; such alone will shake the gates of hell and set up the kingdom of heaven on earth. God does nothing but in answer to prayer."

—JOHN WESLEY

"Now to Him who is able to do far more abundantly beyond all that we ask or think, according to the power that works within us, to Him be the glory in the church and in Christ Jesus to all generations forever and ever. Amen."

—EPHESIANS 3:20–21

When we pray we want God to answer in a notice-able way. However, if we pray and we seldom, if ever, hear from God or feel a sense of His presence, we may need to examine what we believe about prayer, and even what we believe about the One to whom we speak.

The previous verses, from Paul's letter to the Ephesians, confirm that God "is able to do far more abundantly beyond all that we ask or think." That sounds pretty extravagant, but throughout Scripture God has made His power and ability clear.

If creation in the Book of Genesis isn't impressive enough—making everything and everyone from nothing—almost every book from Exodus to Revelation refers to the unmatched power of God. God wants us to know what He is capable of and to remember the mighty deeds He has done. God brought the children of Israel out of Egypt, with signs and wonders such as parting the Red Sea. Remembering what He has done in the past is so important that we will cover it more extensively in chapter three.

God explained His escape plan to an incredulous Moses standing by a bush "burning with fire" that "was not consumed" (Exodus 3:2). The Book of Exodus demonstrates God's interest in and love for His people. He heard their cries (3:7–9), chose Moses for an impossible mission (3:10), and listened to Moses' excuses without giving up on him. His interaction with Moses also shows the patience and understanding our Father has for us. I was so encouraged by this example in my own life.

When I recommitted my life to Jesus at age 17, having origi-
nally confessed faith at 7 years of age, I had one caveat: "Please
don't ask me to pray in public." God doesn't allow caveats; it is
all or nothing with Him. He also has a sense of humor. I found
this out years later when He called me into full-time prayer
ministry and ultimately placed me in the position of national
prayer coordinator for the Southern Baptist Convention.

It was my great joy, though, after surrendering control to
Him, to find that God's grace through His Holy Spirit empowered me to stand, pray, and serve Him. His mercies are new
every morning. Great is Your faithfulness (Lamentations 3:23).

God is not interested in our excuses. He equips those He
calls. In light of my own misgivings about praying in public and
leading others to pray, I developed a lot more sympathy for
Moses in his reluctance (see Exodus 3:11, 13; 4:1, 10). It is no
accident that God recorded the good, bad, and the ugly in His
Word. He knows what we are made of, and He knew we would
need the encouragement of knowing that He used ordinary
people to do extraordinary things. He still does; God has not
changed. What is God calling you to do?

The whole Bible reveals how great and powerful God is, and
the better we know His ways, the more confidence we have to
approach Him about anything and everything. We can pray as
Moses did, "Now therefore, I pray You, if I have found favor
in Your sight, *let me know Your ways that I may know You,*
so that I may find favor in Your sight" (Exodus 33:13, author's

emphasis). Deeper intimacy with Him develops as we know His ways — character — better and grow to know Him more personally. This leads to complete dependence on God and obedient usefulness in His kingdom.

GOD IS IN CONTROL

Studying the Bible is a great way to get to know God's ways. Throughout Scripture, He demonstrates that He is in control. He uses heroes, such as Noah, Abraham, Isaac, Jacob, Joseph, Moses, Joshua, Deborah, Gideon, and Esther, in the Old Testament, to display how He accomplishes His purposes with power through ordinary people like us.

One of my favorite Bible heroes is Daniel. His book overflows with exciting examples of God's powerful control. In the very beginning, we observe that "The Lord *gave* Jehoiakim king of Judah into his hand" (Daniel 1:2, author's emphasis). God was not surprised by the siege in Judah; rather, He caused King Nebuchadnezzer to capture Judah because of Judah's sins. God was in control.

Providentially, Daniel was chosen to be taken into the Babylonian king's personal service team along with three of his friends, Hananiah, Mishael, and Azariah—renamed by the commander of the officials and better known as Shadrach, Meshach, and Abednego. From the beginning of the three-year training program for the chosen youth of Israel, including Daniel and his friends, "Daniel made up his mind that he would not defile himself with the king's choice food or with the wine which he drank" (1:8). Again we see God was in control: "Now *God granted* Daniel favor and compassion in the sight of the commander of the officials" (1:9, author's emphasis).

God showed Himself powerful on behalf of the four young men in their test with a diet of vegetables and water, "And as for these four youths, *God gave* them knowledge and intelligence in every branch of literature and wisdom; Daniel even understood all kinds of visions and dreams" (1:17, author's emphasis). When presented to the king at the end of the training time, these four stood head and shoulders above their peers, and they were chosen to serve in "the king's personal service" (1:19).

God is able to place whomever He wants in whatever position He wants, and He is able to equip them for every good work. Consider the likelihood of four Hebrew men as counselors to the king of Babylon—humanly impossible, but with God it was not only possible but easy.

The adventure crescendos when the king, in frustration over his magicians', conjurers', and sorcerers' inability to reveal his dream or its interpretation, ordered all the wise men—including the four youths—to be killed immediately (2:13).

One can sense the tension of the situation when Daniel asked Arioch, the captain of the king's bodyguard, "For what reason is the decree from the king so urgent?" (2:15). Once he knew it was about a dream, Daniel asked the king to give him a chance to reveal and interpret the dream.

First, though, Daniel went home to inform his friends and pray with Shadrach, Meshach, and Abednego, to ask the God of heaven to reveal the mystery so they wouldn't be destroyed. Believing, faith-filled prayer, focused on God, calmed them and assured them that God was in control and would prevail.

Then the mystery was revealed to Daniel in a dream. Daniel praised God, recognizing that God had answered their prayers, that God removes kings and establishes kings, and that it was God who had revealed the meaning behind the king's dreams.

Answered prayer is about God showing His greatness. Daniel credited God for the revealed wisdom (2:28). He told the king that it was God in heaven who reveals mysteries, and He was giving the king insight about future events. Impressively, King Nebuchadnezzar recognized and admitted to Daniel, "Surely your God is a God of gods and a Lord of kings and a revealer of mysteries, since you have been able to reveal this mystery" (2:47).

In God's plan, Daniel was promoted and his request that his three friends would be allowed to join him for provincial administration in the king's court was granted. God gave them favor for His purposes and for His glory.

NOTHING IS IMPOSSIBLE WITH GOD

This action-packed, adventurous story continued with another most notable, death-defying situation showing God's power. In chapter 3, King Nebuchadnezzar made a golden image for people to worship—or face death in a furnace of blazing fire.

Some Chaldeans, jealous of the administrative positions Shadrach, Meshach, and Abednego held, brought charges against them to King Nebuchadnezzar. He was furious and gave orders to have the young Hebrew men brought to him. He offered them a chance to worship the golden image. But Shadrach, Meshach, and Abednego told the king their God was able to deliver them. They said even if He didn't, they would rather die than serve the king's gods or worship the golden image he had set up. The king sent them to the furnace (3:16–18).

The furnace was seven times hotter than normal and consumed the guards. God not only protected Shadrach, Meshach, and Abednego in the fiery furnace—He joined them there. The king, in amazement at seeing *four* men walking about inside the flaming fire, asked them to come out. The three Hebrew youth did come out and showed no sign of burn or even a scent of smoke! Only God could perform such a miracle, and He did it powerfully (3:19–27.)

Nebuchadnezzar, the pagan king, had to admit that the God of Shadrach, Meshach, and Abednego was all they had claimed and that no other god was able to deliver in such a way. God gave attention to the faith He saw exhibited by these three and was pleased to show Himself strong on their behalf. God's glory was then evident even to those who did not believe in Him.

Being called to die for our faith at one time seemed remote in our context, but precious saints have become martyrs for their faith in increasing numbers in more recent times. Jim Elliott is a twentieth-century example of a missionary who gave his life willingly. He said, "He is no fool who gives what he cannot keep to gain that which he cannot lose."

God is in control, and we need to be surrendered totally to Him. If we live, glory to God; if we die, we go to be with Jesus (see Philippians 1:21). We win either way. He bought us with the blood of Jesus. His plans are good, and He is able to do whatever He wants.

Nebuchadnezzar learned the hard way that God can do whatever He wants. He had another dream, and when Daniel warned him to repent and recognize that the Most High was ruler over the realm of mankind, the king didn't listen. Just "twelve months later he was walking on the roof of the royal palace of Babylon. The king reflected and said, 'Is this not Babylon the great, which I myself have built as a royal residence by the might of my power and for the glory of my majesty?'" (Daniel 4:29–30). God quickly answered and told him from heaven that his sovereignty had just been removed from him.

God is able to exalt a king and to dethrone him. Nebuchadnezzar believed that he was responsible for his success, but after his interaction with God, he learned the hard way that God sets up kings and removes them (Proverbs 8:15; Isaiah 40:22–23). Setting up and removing kings and powers are humanly impossible; however, with God, it is not only possible but easy.

Only God could have brought about such a change in this king, and He used a very creative punishment in the process. He banished the king to the pasture to eat grass like the cattle for seven years until his heart softened and his pride left him. What Nebuchadnezzar learned is vital for us as well. God is able to humble those who walk in pride.

God is compassionate, though, and after a time He restored Nebuchadnezzar's kingdom to him. The king then had a different attitude in Daniel 4:37, "Now I, Nebuchadnezzar, praise, exalt and honor the King of heaven, for all His works are true and His ways just, and He is able to humble those who walk in pride."

Although he had to be aware of all that happened to Nebuchadnezzar, Belshazzar violated the Lord's house. He brought its golden vessels out for him and his guests to use for drinking at a party, soon after he became king. God is alert to these kinds of offenses, and we see another example of the creativity of our God in His judgment.

*Suddenly the fingers of a man's hand emerged
and began writing opposite the lampstand on*

the plaster of the wall of the king's palace, and the king saw the back of the hand that did the writing. The king's face grew pale, and his thoughts alarmed him, and his hip joints went slack and his knees began knocking together (Daniel 5:5–6).

We can imagine the fear and anxiety in that room since, no doubt, a hand writing on a wall would seize your attention.

When Daniel was brought before this king to read the inscription, notice the sobering reality that God displayed in what He wrote on the wall, "God has numbered your kingdom and put an end to it . . . *you have been weighed on the scales and found deficient* . . . your kingdom has been divided and given over to the Medes and the Persians" (5:26, author's emphasis).

God is a God of justice, "There is no authority except from God, and those which exist are established by God" (Romans 13:1). The short reign of Belshazzar ended that very night when he was slain. God sets up and removes authorities without a problem. He is fully in control, and nothing is impossible for Him.

A GOD WHO EXCEEDS
ALL OUR EXPECTATIONS

God gave Daniel favor with the next king as well. Darius appointed Daniel to be one of the three commissioners over the 120 satraps over the kingdom (Daniel 6). Daniel again succeeded and rose above the other commissioners and satraps because of his integrity and dependence on God. When the king planned to appoint him over the entire kingdom, that human frailty—jealousy—reared its ugly head again.

The other commissioners and satraps plotted together to trick the king and trap Daniel into trouble with the king (sounds like the twenty-first century marketplace or government). How would we respond, knowing the same God?

The commissioners and other high officials plotted ways they could get rid of Daniel, but they did not consider Daniel's God. They came up with a scheme that the king should establish a statute that for 30 days anyone who petitioned any god or man besides the king would be cast into the lions' den.

Daniel, knowing the new injunction, remained faithful to his normal prayertimes. The villains seemed to have won when they approached the king about Daniel disobeying the injunction. The tension rose again as the distressed king realized his decree could not be revoked; Daniel would, by that decree, go to the lions' den (6:12–15).

Daniel's faithfulness to his God and excellence in his service so impressed the king that he said to Daniel, before he sent him to the lion's den, "Your God whom you constantly serve will Himself deliver you" (6:16). That is quite a statement for a pagan king and it illustrates how God gives favor and sometimes even gives a faithful follower influence in a secular world.

The king may have made a positive statement seemingly expressing faith, but he spent the night restless, and at the break of day, he raced to the lions' den. He was anxious to know if Daniel was still alive. Daniel answered and assured him that God had vindicated him since he was innocent before God. There was no injury at all to Daniel. Only God could have kept the lions calm.

Again the pagan king Darius praised God and said that men were to fear and tremble before the God of Daniel. Darius acknowledged Him as the living God who delivered Daniel. God noticeably displayed His ability to exceed all our expectations. *This* is the God we approach in prayer!

The Old Testament is full of stories like these with nail-biting tension between the faithful and the villains who continually try to trip up God's chosen ones. Even these pagan kings recognized that the living God is all-powerful. The more familiar we become with the Bible record showing God's power, the easier it will be to pray with belief.

Looking back at these stories in the Book of Daniel, we are reminded of some of God's ways.

- He appoints nations to capture His people to discipline them and draw their attention back to Him.
- He opens doors for those who trust in Him.
- He equips those He calls to serve.
- He protects His servants from evildoers' plans.

- He removes kings and appoints whom He pleases.
- He causes even pagans to acknowledge that He alone is God.
- He will be exalted above all gods.
- He is righteous and just, and He takes action against evil.
- He is tenderhearted, having compassion (even on Nebuchadnezzar after disciplining him).

You may remember other characteristics of God from the Book of Daniel. List them in the margin here or in your journal. (If you are not using a journal, this may be a good time to start.)

JESUS, GOD'S ULTIMATE POWER

In the New Testament, God's ability came to a major high point with the birth of Jesus, demonstrating His purposeful control even further. When the angel Gabriel visited Mary to tell her that she had been chosen to give birth to the Messiah, she was willing but puzzled about how that could be, since she was a virgin. Gabriel answered simply, "For nothing will be impossible with God" (Luke 1:37).

She wisely rested in that knowledge and beautifully praised God her Savior, in what is called the Magnificat (Luke 1:46–55). God's ways are not always what we expect—the King was born in a manger, and He rode a donkey colt into Jerusalem as foretold in Zechariah 9:9. Because of the price Jesus paid on the

Cross for our sins, we are no longer separated from God and can now come to Him in prayer.

Jesus, God incarnate, demonstrated his power over the waves of the sea (Mark 4:35–41); over medical conditions (Mark 1:29–34); over death (John 11:38–44); and in salvation (Matthew 19:16–26). I especially like a story that gives us insight into how Jesus responds when we pray as if we don't know the power of the One that we're consulting. This story, found in Mark 9:14–29, clearly shows that nothing is impossible with God.

A father had brought his demonically possessed son to the disciples, but they were unable to cast out the demon. Then Jesus walked up to ask what the commotion was about. The father answered Jesus' questions about the boy and said to Him, "*If* You can do anything, take pity on us and help us" (9:22, author's emphasis). This is where we hear the exasperation of Jesus, "'*If* You can? All things are possible to him who believes'" (9:23).

Through this exchange, Jesus used the teachable moment to explain to His disciples that there are some things God will do only in response to our prayers. Jesus told them, "'This kind cannot come out by anything but prayer'" (9:29). He reinforced the importance of prayer and fasting, and the disciples learned that casting out demons had less to do with technique and more to do with their relationship with God. This kind of prayer is, after all, calling on God and believing in His power.

Jesus helps us make the transition from the Old Testament to the New Testament and into the church age, in which prayer plays such a prominent role. God is able to do anything He wants to and instructs us to pray with that in mind. As we approach God in prayer, we need to remember that He is our creator, and He is all-powerful.

We will pray well when we learn to listen to the One with the wisdom and the plan for eternity. A great promise to memorize is, "Greater is He who is in you than he who is in the world" (1 John 4:4).

Only God could have come up with the plan to send Jesus to take the sins of the world on Himself, and He carried it out perfectly. Jesus died on the Cross to conquer sin and death. After three days He rose again and walked among witnesses for 40 days before He ascended back into heaven (Acts 1:9–10; 1 Corinthians 15:3–6). Jesus was obedient to the point of death so we can have a relationship with Him to accomplish God's remaining purposes (Philippians 2:8).

Time is getting short before Jesus comes again, and God is looking for those who will obey the Great Commission (Matthew 28:18–20). Remember His word recorded by John, "We must work the works of [God] who sent [Jesus] as long as it is day; night is coming when no one can work" (John 9:4). There is much to be done and prayer is foundational to all God gives us to do.

Our prayers begin best with worship, so that our focus stays on the supremacy of the One to whom we speak. One way to come before God with intentional awe and reverence for His holiness and majesty is by praying Scripture. For example, we can pray a paraphrase of Revelation 4:8–11 with the heavenly living creatures.

Praising God for who He is takes us into His throne room and banishes the devil who hates praise of God. Also, after any time of praising and worshipping God, we are more aware that the God we're addressing in prayer is the same One "that is able to do exceed abundantly above all that we ask or think" (Ephesians 3:20 KJV).

Pray with Me

Father,

You are holy, holy, holy. You are the Lord God, the Almighty, the One who was and who is and who is to come. In light of Your majesty, Lord, we bow down before You. Worthy are You, our Lord and our God to receive glory and honor and power. For You created all things, and because of Your will all things came into existence. Keep our focus on You and Your glory as we learn to pray the way You desire.

In Jesus' name we pray, amen.

For Further Study

Read Jeremiah 32:16–42.

• What do we learn about God's character from Jeremiah's prayer and God's answer in these verses?

• Make a list of God's attributes in these verses.

• What caused God to bring calamity on the people of Israel in verse 23 and 33?

• What was God's purpose in bringing judgment on His people in verses 38–39?

Read 1 Samuel 17.

• Why was David on the battlefield? See verses 17–19.

• Whose reputation was he concerned about in verses 26 and 36?

• How was God glorified by David in verses 46–47?

• What are some other Bible stories that demonstrate the character and power of God on behalf of His people?

• What is your favorite one?

• What are some of the characteristics about God that stand out to you from this chapter?

CHAPTER TWO

OVERCOMING OBSTACLES
WE BRING TO PRAYER

"Prayer is interpersonal communication between two individuals. In Scripture, it matters far less *how*, *when* and *what* you say than how well you know him to whom you pray."

—W. BINGHAM HUNTER

"If your praise has been interrupted for any reason, would you restart it? Praise God for just giving us Jesus. Why? Because He is unequaled in His position, undisputed in His power, and unrivaled in His praise. He is worthy of all your praise 24/7!"

—ANNE GRAHAM LOTZ

"Prayer is an unnatural activity; alien to our proud human nature. Yet, when we slow down to pray, we become astonished by God's approachability, endeared by his care, stilled by his presence, encouraged by his affirmation, and challenged by his insatiable desire to make the truth known. Perfect peace comes only through relating with the Peacemaker himself."

—BILL HYBELS

"Do not quench the Spirit."

—1 THESSALONIANS 5:19

"Do not grieve the Holy Spirit of God, by whom you were sealed for the day of redemption."

—EPHESIANS 4:30

When I was the national prayer coordinator for Southern Baptists, working at the North American Mission Board (NAMB), I held periodic meetings with prayer coordinators from around North America from a cross section of venues—state or province, associational, and local church. Those were exciting meetings as I heard what they needed in the field, enjoyed their interaction, and especially enjoyed our prayer times together.

At one such meeting, we were to discuss the NAMB prayer website. The technical support team had helped me set up in a conference room with a plethora of cords and connections to the projector and computer. It was an all-day meeting, and I didn't plan to use my laptop until after lunch. So I pushed the pause button on the projector and went ahead with a devotion and an extended time of sharing and prayer.

After a lovely luncheon, I finally moved into the website evaluation. I had barely gotten started, maybe 15 minutes, when a message popped up saying my battery was low and the computer was going into hibernation.

JESUS IS OUR POWER SOURCE

With all the cords lying around, I thought my computer was plugged into an electrical outlet; it was not. I went scurrying to get a cord brought in and connected. Once the electrical cord was plugged in, the computer worked fine. This was a timely illustration because, providentially, our devotion Scripture had been, "[God] is able to do far more abundantly beyond all that we ask or think, *according to the power that works within us*" (Ephesians 3:20, author's emphasis). The laptop also works according to the power within it.

Do we ever get so caught up in our rituals of the Christian life that, like the laptop battery, we *seem* to be working fine? We can do good things in the flesh for a while, but then we burn out. Our battery goes dead. It is only when we are clean before God, depending on His strength alone, that we truly pray and work effectively. His power working in us is able to keep us humming along, even excelling in our Christian growth and usefulness.

By Paul's admonition to the Thessalonians, "Do not quench the Spirit," we realize that we are able to quench or thwart the working of the Holy Spirit in our prayers and in our lives (1 Thessalonians 5:19). We can bring obstacles to prayer unintentionally.

Sin is the culprit.

> *Behold, the LORD's hand is not so short that it cannot save; nor His ear so dull that it cannot hear. But your iniquities have made a separation between you and your God, and your sins have hidden His face from you so that He does not hear* (Isaiah 59:1–2).

THE BIGGEST OBSTACLE

The biggest obstacle to effective prayer is lacking a personal relationship with Jesus. The Apostle John recorded these words of Jesus, "I am the way, and the truth, and the life; no one comes to the Father but through Me" (John 14:6). Once we are related to Jesus, He covers us with His righteousness so that we can freely talk with our heavenly Father.

This obstacle has arisen because too many well-intentioned people have walked an aisle, repeated the words of a prayer, or joined a church, but they have never understood what it truly means to be a Christ follower. Those persons may well believe that they are Christians, but they do not have a *love relationship with Christ.*

After reading John 2:23–24 at a "Secret Church" meeting, missions leader and author David Platt said, "Jesus observed many who saw the miracles He did, but He knew they were not true believers. . . . Is there a word for us? Such self-proclaimed Christians are deluded; there are a whole lot of people who think they are saved and are not!"

Much of the problem of ineffective churches in our day may go back to the practice whereby many churches have welcomed new church members without making sure they are believers. God does not call us to join a church, attend worship services, and thereby think that we are good Christians. Listen to the words Jesus spoke to His disciples right before He ascended back to heaven:

"Go therefore and make disciples of all the nations, baptizing them in the name of the Father and the Son and the Holy Spirit, teaching them *to observe all that I commanded you; and lo, I am with you always, even to the end of the age"* (Matthew 28:19–20, author's emphasis).

Jesus wants us to develop as disciples, those who take following Him seriously enough to surrender our very lives to His purposes. Disciples learn everything they can about their Master's character, along with His commandments or requirements, so that they can emulate, obey, and bring honor and glory to Him.

If this resonates with your experience and you desire to surrender yourself now to God's purposes described above, I invite you to pray your own version of the following right now.

Dear God,

I have been trying to be a Christian in my own strength, and it is not working. I know that I am a sinner and need a Savior. I believe that You sent Jesus to be my Savior, and right now, I ask You, Jesus to take control of my life, to be my Savior and Lord. I repent of trying to live my life my own way and I surrender my life to You. Please take me into Your family and fill me with the Holy Spirit to enable me to live for You alone.

If you are sincerely praying this prayer, be sure to tell someone very soon about your decision to trust only Jesus for eternal life.

If you confess with your mouth Jesus as Lord, and believe in your heart that God raised Him from the dead, you will be saved; for with the heart a person believes, resulting in righteousness, and with the mouth he confesses, resulting in salvation (Romans 10:9–10).

BLIND SPOTS AND COMFORTABLE SINS

There are some sins that we may no longer notice because tolerance and societal approval have made them acceptable. There are some not-so-subtle sins of the Ten Commandments variety that we are not dealing with in this book. But depending on your age and biblical literacy, some of the sins listed by Paul in 1 Corinthians 6:9–11 may be surprising to you.

Or do you not know that the unrighteous will not inherit the kingdom of God? Do not be deceived; neither fornicators, nor idolaters, nor adulterers, nor effeminate, nor homosexuals, nor thieves, nor the covetous, nor drunkards, nor revilers, nor swindlers, will inherit the kingdom of God.

If any of these sins exist in your life, repent before God and turn away from them. Then you can embrace Paul's words in verse 11, "Such were some of you; but you were washed, but you were sanctified, but you were justified in the name of the Lord Jesus Christ and in the Spirit of our God."

As active, churchgoing believers, we may not be bothered with those kinds of blatant sins, but we may have developed blind spots. We may have become so comfortable with a socially acceptable sin that we are either numb to it or no longer think of it as sin. Sins of any kind block the empowering flow of God's Spirit within us. Therefore, it is important to address them for what they are.

There is sin in the Christian camp today, and that is holding back the great victories that God so longs to give us. He is looking for a consecrated people "that He may strongly support those whose heart is completely His" (2 Chronicles 16:9). We will talk more about consecration in the next chapter.

Paul's words to the Ephesian church, which was growing in spite of the decadent culture around them, instruct us today: "Do not participate in the unfruitful deeds of darkness, but instead even expose them; for it is disgraceful even to speak of the things which are done by them in secret" (5:11–12). The more immoral our society becomes, the more different we are called to be, the more we need the Light of the world to shine brightly through us.

Our objective is clearly stated by Peter: But you are A CHOSEN RACE, A royal PRIESTHOOD, A HOLY NATION, A PEOPLE FOR God's OWN POSSESSION, so that you may proclaim the excellencies of Him who has called you out of darkness into His marvelous light" (1 Peter 1:9)

In our politically correct society, we are called on continually to stop being so rigid and to tolerate other people's beliefs and affirm their right to have them. What are the blind spots that trip us up? What are the comfortable sins that cause us to compromise our faith and quench the Spirit?

PRAYERLESSNESS

Beatrice wanted to follow her Savior. She had good intentions to read her Bible and pray each day. However, she was the mother of two young children, and her husband was overseas on a military assignment. Fatigue set in pretty quickly as she tried to balance the demands of cooking, cleaning, teaching, and caring for children, along with the equally challenging chore of balancing the budget. She just didn't seem to have the time to pray. We can empathize with her and will discuss her solution in the next chapter.

One of the biggest ways we quench the Spirit is by not praying at all. This is an easy trap when we let the demands of work or home responsibilities monopolize our time day after day. Without intentionally setting aside a definite quiet time to focus only on God, we can drift away from depending on His direction and go our own way. It can be a very subtle shift away from the narrow path on which God is leading us to follow Him.

Isaiah 59:14–16 reads like today's newspaper.

> *Justice is turned back . . . righteousness stands far away . . . truth has stumbled in the street . . . Now the LORD saw, and it was displeasing in His sight that there was no justice. And He saw that there was no man, and was astonished that there was no one to intercede.*

In Ezekiel 22:29–30 we can also hear our Father's lament over prayerlessness.

> *The people of the land have practiced oppression and committed robbery, and they have wronged the poor and needy and have oppressed the sojourner without justice. I searched for a man among them who should build up the wall and stand in the gap before Me for the land, that I would not destroy it; but I found no one.*

Prayerlessness is a result of living one's life independent of God. It is just the opposite of trusting the Lord with all one's heart, as described in Proverbs 3:5–6. Instead, one simply trusts his or her own understanding. Jerry Bridges calls this *ungodliness* in his book, *Respectable Sins.*

> Ungodliness may be defined as living one's everyday life with little or no thought of God, or of God's will, or of God's glory, or of one's dependence on God. You can readily see, then, that someone can lead a respectable life and still be ungodly in the sense that God is essentially irrelevant in his or her life. We rub shoulders with such people every day in the course of our ordinary activities. They may be friendly, courteous, and helpful to other people, but God is not at all in their thoughts. They may even attend church for an hour or so each week but then live the remainder of the week as if God doesn't exist. They are not wicked people, but they are ungodly.

Prayerlessness and ungodliness are birthed from the same omission of the leadership role God warrants in our lives.

Sadly, prayerlessness in believers' lives is not new. In Isaiah 43:21–24 God says to "the people whom [He] formed for" Himself, "Yet you have not called on Me, O Jacob; but you have become weary of Me, O Israel . . . Rather you have burdened Me with your sins, you have wearied Me with your iniquities."

In our day, when we consider that Jesus is the Head of the church and God is the One with all wisdom, why *don't* we pray without ceasing? We'll consider how to do that in the next chapter. God was searching for an intercessor in biblical days and continues to have difficulty finding one today.

FORGETFULNESS

Forgetfulness leads to disobedience. The author of Judges shows us, "The sons of Israel did what was evil in the sight of the LORD, and *forgot* the LORD their God" (3:7, author's emphasis). The psalmist gives us another example of how forgetfulness and disobedience go together. "The sons of Ephraim . . . did not keep the covenant of God and refused to walk in His law; they *forgot* His deeds and His miracles that He had shown them" (Psalm 78:9–11, author's emphasis).

God gives us a warning against forgetfulness, especially when we are successful—when God gives us prosperity and ease in this life. It follows the greatest commandment, quoted later by Jesus, "And you shall love the LORD your God with all your heart and with all your soul and with all your might" (Deuteronomy 6:5). A few verses later, He describes the privileges and blessings likely to come and then gives His warning in verse 12, "Then watch yourself, that you do not *forget* the LORD who brought you from the land of Egypt, out of the house of slavery" (author's emphasis).

After God commands them to instruct their children about God's ways and promises, He gives another warning that tells us why it is so important to remember the Lord and His commandments, "So the LORD commanded us to observe all these statutes, to fear the LORD our God *for our good*" (6:24–25, author's emphasis).

God is not telling us to remember what He has done because He has an ego problem; rather, it is *for our good*. Reflecting on the mighty deeds God has done in the past gives us faith to trust Him with the future completely. We can avoid the unhealthy emotions of stress, anxiety, and fear by remembering who He is and what He has done. Things also go better for us when we remember that *He* is God and we are not.

Forgetfulness is very serious with our covenant-keeping God. We hear His warning in Deuteronomy 8:19–20,

> *It shall come about if you ever forget the LORD your God and go after other gods and serve them and worship them, I testify against you today that you will surely perish . . . because you would not listen to the voice of the LORD your God"* (author's emphasis).

If you find yourself forgetting God's greatness and falling into worry and anxiety, think about how easily we can memorize a worry by meditating on or thinking about it repeatedly. Instead of worrying, we can use that ability and realign our focus to "let the word of Christ richly dwell within [us]" (Colossians 3:16). Yes, we *can* memorize Scripture, and that will make it easier to *listen to God* and for "the peace of God [to] rule in our hearts" (v. 15). You may have heard the expression, "Glance at the problem; gaze at God."

Proverbs 3:1–2 provides helpful instruction for us, "My son, *do not forget* my teaching, but let your heart keep my commandments; for length of days and years of life and peace they will add to you" (author's emphasis).

Unforgiveness

Unforgiveness is a big problem among Christians today, and that may be why Jesus warned about it frequently in His teachings. There are two sides to unforgiveness. The first is the lack of confession and repentance from our specific sins, asking God for His forgiveness. Jesus began His earthly ministry by saying, "Repent, for the kingdom of heaven is at hand" (Matthew 4:17). The second involves other people failing to ask for or to give forgiveness when we have wronged them or they have wronged us. Harboring unforgiveness allows a deep root of bitterness to develop and stymie our prayer life.

The author of Hebrews instructs,

Pursue peace with all men, and the sanctification without which no one will see the Lord. See to it that no one comes short of the grace of God; that no root of bitterness springing up causes trouble, and by it many be defiled (12:14–15).

Paul also speaks to the importance of turning loose of unforgiveness in his letter to the Ephesians,

Let all bitterness and wrath and anger and clamor and slander be put away from you, along with all malice. And be kind to one another, tender-hearted, forgiving each other, just as God in Christ also has forgiven you (4:31–32).

Often it is an insignificant thing that first starts friction between people. However, when it is allowed to fester and other small irritations are added, the buildup causes people to lose all perspective. Unforgiveness sets in between the parties involved. It is vital that we keep short accounts with both God and man.

The devil loves to stir up trouble and to get us to be against each other instead of against him, our real enemy. We need to be alert to his devious tactics of division, trying to create disunity between Christ and us or between us and a fellow Christian.

When we consider the price Jesus paid on the Cross because of our sins, we realize that we have sinned against God to a far worse degree than anything another person could ever do to us. It does not come naturally to forgive, but we can ask God to empower us to forgive the seemingly unforgiveable.

It is a matter of surrender to His better way. Remember the words of Jesus on the Cross, "Father, forgive them; for they do not know what they are doing" (Luke 23:34). One of the core values at my church is, "We want to be more and more like Jesus." Forgiving when it does not seem fair, as Jesus did, is a powerful witness to believers and unbelievers alike. When we release our right to be right, amazing freedom floods our soul and we can turn it loose.

My daddy told me one time when I was a child that my anger and lack of desire to forgive my friend only hurt me. He reminded me that I was the one obsessing about how she needed to say she was sorry, and she didn't even seem to know she had done anything wrong. I had to really pray about that because I thought I was right.

Daddy encouraged me to ask Jesus to help me turn it loose and forgive my friend. I finally did ask Jesus for help, and an amazing thing happened. The next time I talked to my friend, I found that I really liked her again and wanted to hang out with her.

We may get older, but how similar are we as adults to this childlike example, in our resistance to forgiving others for the offenses of daily interaction? This one sin can have eternal significance because when unforgiveness is rampant in the body of Christ, our witness for the Lord is hindered. Paul tells us, "Be angry, and yet do not sin; do not let the sun go down on your anger, and do not give the devil an opportunity" (Ephesians 4:26–27).

Those instructive verses were given to Joel and me before we married by a sweet older pastor and his wife, whom I dearly loved and respected. It is a good reminder for all of us because there will be differences of opinion in marriages and other relationships. My mother wisely counseled me to risk losing an argument to gain the relationship. She would ask, "Is it more important to be right or to be in right relationship with your hubby?"

When Peter asked Jesus how often he should forgive his brother, he suggested seven times. But Jesus answered that he should be willing to forgive 70 times 7—or continually (Matthew 18:21–22). Unforgiveness is extensive in our world today with believers bringing lawsuits against each other as a normal way of life. We have truly forgotten the teaching of Jesus.

God sees the injustice in our lives, and He knows the perfect timing for judgment. In Romans, we are commanded to be at peace with all people so far as it depends on us (Romans 12:17-20). We cannot force others to be at peace with us, but we can do our part. When we leave vengeance to God and treat the opposing party with kindness, God can bring conviction to that person so that he or she may be drawn to Jesus.

Paul wrote very sternly about this when he admonished the early believers to settle their differences with each other among themselves rather than take their disagreements to court (1 Corinthians 6:1–7). He says it would be better to be defrauded, emphasizing the importance to forgive each other for the sake of the kingdom of God and our witness to unbelievers.

When we stand before Jesus, those things we thought so important and unforgiveable will pale, as we wish we had lived a better life. It is so freeing to release the emotion before it builds into a root of bitterness (Hebrews 12:15). Ask God to search your heart to see if there is *anyone* with whom you need to make peace—to ask for or offer forgiveness (Romans 12:18).

PRIDE

In the spring of the year, I parked my clean black car in the parking lot of an unfamiliar office building where I was attending a daylong meeting. That afternoon, as I looked for my car, it didn't seem to be there. As I finally used the remote to search, a very yellow, pollen-covered car responded with lights flashing. Just as pollen in the air had polluted my car, pride can pollute our lives unnoticed as we go about our daily lives.

How do we feel when someone cuts in front of us on the highway? Does our prideful awareness of "our rights" kick in? How about when someone worked very hard on a project and a fellow worker received the credit and applause? Is it our pride that needs recognition? As an antidote to pride, we are to "work heartily, as for the Lord" (Colossians 3:23–24). John clarifies that "the boastful pride of life, is not from the Father, but is from the world" (1 John 2:16).

Pride is often in cahoots with unforgiveness because we don't want to admit that we've wronged or failed to forgive someone. *Surely it was not my fault* we think. This is not new. Adam and Eve exhibited this trait when God confronted them about their disobedience in the Garden of Eden: Adam blamed Eve; Eve blamed the serpent (Genesis 3:12–13).

In God's eyes we are each responsible for our own choices and will ultimately answer to Him for our actions. Jesus said that those who did evil deeds will be raised to a "resurrection of judgment" (John 5:29).

Second Chronicles 26 gives us an example of one who "did right in the sight of the LORD": King Uzziah (26:4). The chronicler tells us, "as long as he sought the Lord, God prospered him" (26:5). However, "when he became strong, his heart was so proud that he acted corruptly, and he was unfaithful to the LORD his God" (26:16). God's judgment was swift—King Uzziah became a leper and died in that state.

Pride is subtle and we can all fall into its trap, so it is important to be alert. Proverbs 16:18–19 offers a wise warning, "Pride goes before destruction, and a haughty spirit before stumbling. It is better to be of a humble spirit with the lowly, than to divide the spoil with the proud."

The most committed Christian leader can fall into the trap of people pleasing. Pride rises up and loves to receive affirmation, but when we seek approval from the world instead of from our heavenly Father, we get into trouble (see John 5:44). People-pleasing can also lead to a subtle slide into complacency so that we don't offend *anyone*. Either one of these will take us away from being consecrated to our Lord for His use.

When we choose to do things our own way instead of God's way, it is our pride getting in the way of wisdom. Eve fell into its trap when she listened to Satan and ate the fruit. Peter gives us the antidote to pride: "Therefore humble yourselves under the mighty hand of God, that He may exalt you at the proper time" (1 Peter 5:6). We can trust God's timing; His approval is what we really want. Paul says, "For it is not he who commends himself that is approved, but he whom the Lord commends" (2 Corinthians 10:18).

Jesus exposes the Pharisees, and us, "You receive glory from one another and you do not seek the glory that is from the one and only God" (John 5:44). Who are we trying to please, and whose glory are we seeking? Pride is insidious and can keep us from humbling ourselves before God in prayer.

Disobedience

God gave the children of Israel the Ten Commandments "in order that the fear of [God] may remain with [them], so that [they] may not sin" (Exodus 20:20). They were noticeably fearful to the point of asking Moses to talk to God and then report to them what He said, as they were afraid to speak with God themselves.

Moses was on Mount Sinai for a long time getting God's commands and the two tablets of stone that God had written on (31:18), when God declared, "They have quickly turned aside from the way which I commanded them. They have made for themselves a molten calf, and have worshiped it" (Exodus 32:8). Forgetfulness and disobedience go hand-in-hand.

Ignorance is not bliss when it comes to knowing God's commands, which we are to obey. Believers are expected to know the requirements of our Lord, found in the Bible. Jesus gave us specific instructions in His Great Commission: "Make disciples . . . teaching them to observe all that I commanded you" (Matthew 28:19–20). Disciples of Christ learn God's laws.

What if we were stopped by a highway patrol officer for driving too fast? Would our response that we didn't know the speed limit sway his decision about giving us a speeding ticket? His response would probably be to point out the obvious road signs with the speed limit posted. In order to enjoy the privilege of driving, we must know and obey the related laws of the land.

We can expect to pay the penalty if we disobey earthly highway laws, so how much more can we expect to pay a penalty if we disobey God? Paul explains in the first chapter of Romans that God provided obvious "road signs" in creation that demonstrate that He is God and He is in control. If disobedience becomes a habit, we line up for God giving us over to our sinful passions (Romans 1:24–32). Willful disobedience to God will not get a pass and is very serious to Him. It's another word for *sin*.

God reminds us,

> As obedient children, do not be conformed to
> the former lusts which were yours in your igno-
> rance, but like the Holy One who called you,
> be holy yourselves also in all your behavior;
> because it is written, "YOU SHALL BE HOLY, FOR
> I AM HOLY." If you address as Father the One
> who impartially judges according to each one's
> work, conduct yourselves in fear during the
> time of your stay on earth (1 Peter 1:14–17).

UNBELIEF

Unbelief will stymie prayer and is a serious heart problem that
we are warned sternly about in Hebrews, "Take care, brethren,
that there not be in any one of you an evil, unbelieving heart
that falls away from the living God" (Hebrews 3:12). Through
the writer of Hebrews, God reminds us of the hardness of heart
experienced by the children of Israel released from Egyptian
captivity, how the older generation was not allowed to enter the
Promised Land because of their unbelief.

Unbelief hinders the power of God. When Jesus visited
His hometown, He did no great miracles there because of their
unbelief (Mark 6:1–6). In another setting,

He reproached [His eleven disciples] for their unbelief and hardness of heart, because they had not believed those who had first seen Him after He had risen. And He said to them "Go into all the world and preach the gospel to all creation. He who has believed and has been baptized shall be saved; but he who has disbelieved shall be condemned (Mark 16:14–16, author's emphasis).

God takes unbelief very seriously indeed. However, unbelief is another subtle sin that we can overlook if we are not careful. God still works miracles in our midst whether or not we realize it. Paul speaks to this, "What then? If some did not believe, their unbelief will not nullify the faithfulness of God, will it?" (Romans 3:3)

With our logical minds, we express unbelief when we fail to give credit to God when He performs a miracle, such as a changed life or a healed body. Our prayers are definitely hindered by unbelief, and we can slip into disbelief that God is in control by focusing on our personal circumstances or the world news.

Remember the father of the demonic son who brought his son to the disciples and ultimately to Jesus? That father exhibited some faith just by coming to Jesus. When Jesus said, "All things are possible to him who believes" (Mark 9:23), the man cried out and said, "I do believe; help my unbelief" (9:24). We want to believe, but we, too, may need to ask God to help us fully believe.

Unbelief is exhibited by the sin of trying to answer our own prayers for fear God may not answer or that He needs our help. We see this in the story of Abraham and Sarah. They believed God would give them an heir, but they chose to help Him out by using Hagar. The story is in Genesis 15:4–6; 16:1–2.

What we believe about God and His unfathomable ability will be displayed in the way we pray. Are we afraid we may embarrass God if we ask for something too difficult? Or do we boldly ask for impossible healings; for eyes to be opened to believe in Him; for our families, churches, and cities to be changed for His glory? Unbelief is the most serious sin, so stop right now and ask God to search your heart for any area of unbelief. Ask Him to stretch your ability to believe that our Abba Father can do anything!

IDOLATRY IN THE TWENTY-FIRST CENTURY

There are few Christians today who worship literal, sculpted idols, but in their place we have found contemporary idols to replace worship of the One and only Holy God. Like the subtle sins we've been discussing, idols are insidious and hazardous to our faith walk and prayer life.

In our spiritual walk, we must stay alert and not let what we do for God become our focus rather than God. Even prayer can become an idol if we are not alert. Prayer is the conduit to reach God just as a straw is a conduit to drink refreshing water on a hot day. We must be vigilant to worship only God, the One that we reach through prayer. The following are just a few other examples.

BUSYNESS

An aspiration of many Christians is to be seen as busy. "Oh, I'm so busy these days," is a refrain often heard as if to impress the listeners with how important or popular the speaker is. We may be so busy with things God is not calling us to do that we miss the important work that He has for us to do. If we are too busy, we will surely miss blessings God wants to shower on us in our quiet, private communion with Him.

Evaluating our calendar and financial stewardship will help us see where our heart is and how we are spending our Christian lives. Are we being still with God, seeking His direction? Are we bearing eternal fruit? Or are we staying so busy, even doing good things, that we miss God? We have to make hard choices because the world is full of intriguing distractions. Busyness can be an idol and the product of the worldly pride of life.

MATERIAL POSSESSIONS OR "STUFF"

Do we own stuff or does stuff own us? We can become so entangled in acquiring stuff, then storing, organizing, displaying, cleaning, and protecting our stuff that we have little time for anything else. My daddy used to ask Mother as we were nearing home after a long trip, "What if our house burned down while we were gone?" My mother's answer still rings in my ear, "I guess we'll just start over again."

We can enjoy a nice home with heat and indoor plumbing as well as the next person, but we need to remember that God is the One who blesses us with everything we need. It is God who gives us the "power to make wealth" (Deuteronomy 8:18), so we need to be grateful and enjoy His blessings but not be obsessed with, prideful, or anxious about them.

Jesus' words on this topic in Matthew 6:25–32, tell us that we don't have to worry about what we'll wear or what we'll eat because our heavenly Father knows what we need and will provide. A great verse to memorize is Matthew 6:33: "But seek first His kingdom and His righteousness, and all these things will be added to you." Do we believe that?

Ask God to help you hold your stuff with open hands in case He needs to take it away for His purposes. Our grasping and being obsessed with our stuff won't keep it safe if God chooses to remove it for our good, but that attitude can let stuff become our idol.

Hebrews 12:1–2 and Philippians 3:13–14 remind us of the importance of turning loose of anything that entangles us and keeps us from running with endurance the race set before us, so that we can press on toward the upward call of God in Christ Jesus.

GREED

Greed is a root cause of the materialism just discussed. In short, greed is undue desire for something, whether it be for financial gain, for food, or anything that belongs to somebody else. Jesus warned, "Beware, and be on your guard against every form of greed; for not even when one has an abundance does his life consist of his possessions" (Luke 12:15). Greed can lead us to worse sins, even leading some to renounce the Lord (Psalm 10:3). Our heart's desire needs to be examined daily so that we do not insult God. Ask yourself, "Is there anything I want more than God?"

We see just how serious God takes greed in the lives of His people in Joshua 7. After being routed by their enemies at Ai, Joshua mourned and cried out to the Lord, asking why God had brought them into this land to be defeated. But God explained to Joshua that they had experienced the resounding defeat because they had disobeyed Him and had possession of things that the Lord had banned. One of the Israelites, Achan, let greed get the best of him, and when confronted with his sin, he admitted that he coveted beautiful, forbidden items and took them for himself (vv. 20–26). Joshua and the people immediately cleansed the camp by stoning him and destroying the contraband. God's judgment was swift!

To cleanse ourselves we also need to consider our homes. Are there worldly distractions hiding among our belongings, in our hearts or on our minds, that we are greedily holding onto?

Are they competing with God for first place in our lives? Like Joshua's army, in our prayers, we cannot stand victorious over our spiritual enemy until we are fully committed to God.

A ready cure for greed is to "Delight yourself in the LORD; and He will give you the desires of your heart" (Psalm 37:4). Providentially as we delight in the Lord, our heart's desires begin to line up with His will and He delights in answering our God-glorifying prayers.

ENTERTAINMENT

Entertainment is big business in our day, from movies and media to sports and even Christian concerts. We don't want to miss that next great, "once in a lifetime" opportunity to see or enjoy some form of entertainment. Why do you think sports and Hollywood entertainment are thriving? We as a people love to be entertained with bright lights and moving objects.

Sports stars and actors are some of the highest paid individuals in our society because we so greatly value our entertainment. Paul warns, of those that "set their minds on earthly things" (Philippians 3:19). Where do we set our minds? Is God's glory our passion or is it only one among many interests?

Setting one's mind on earthly things can be subtle, such as when, while knowing that sex outside of marriage is wrong and sinful before our Holy God, one watches a movie or TV program that promotes and glamorizes adultery and fornication.

"Oh, it's just a movie," he or she may say to justify watching. But in reality, how far is that from pornography and degradation of one's mind? Have we become numb to the effect?

Remember the little children's song, "Be careful little eyes what you see; be careful little ears what you hear." This is good advice for adults as well. What we see, hear, and say affects our minds, and that is where much sin begins (James 1:14–15).

If we read, study, and memorize God's Word, we will know the truth, which will help us know right from wrong. We can then better discern whether what we read, watch, listen to, or talk about is pleasing to God. We may have to forego some worldly pleasures and entertainment to walk in a manner that brings glory to God.

SUBTLE INFLUENCES IN OUR DAILY LIVES

I mentioned pollen covered my car like a blanket of yellow in the spring, and that happened just because the car was out in the atmosphere. We, too, may start our days clean before God and become contaminated by our environment. Sexually enticing billboards, crude bumper stickers, and violent news on the radio all can contaminate us—just on our commute to work or running errands.

On the stops along our daily routine — our computer, cell phone, our office, medical appointments, cleaners, grocer, drugstore, and schools, we may have interaction with people who don't know Jesus. That may expose us to conversations we would not choose, and they may shock us with an image that tries to stay in our minds. It's not easy being clean.

We must stay alert and continually renew our minds with God's Word. Paul reminds us that we must "lay aside the deeds of darkness" (Romans 13:12). Light dispels darkness and we bring the Light of the world to our situations. We can be a witness to the peace and joy that God gives because we have given our lives to Jesus.

Even in Christian circles, worldly influence can be subtle and corrosive to our walk with Jesus. We meet with goals to study God's Word, to worship Him, to hold one another accountable and encourage each other to be bold to share our faith. Yet, instead, what often become the subjects of our conversations during fellowship times before and after Sunday Bible study or church services?

Depending on the time of year, it could be football, baseball, or some other sport. Or how about that great, well-known speaker that everyone is buzzing about? The adulation that should be given to our Lord is heaped on a person. Hebrews 3:13 is instructive: "But encourage one another day after day, as long as it is still called 'Today,' so that none of you will be hardened by the deceitfulness of sin."

We need to pray and ask God to teach us how to worship Him in spirit and in truth, as the Father is seeking, so that we can—and help others to—keep our focus on Him (John 4:23). Church is a great place to encourage one another in our walk and spiritual growth, to build enthusiasm for being a Christ follower. God may use you and me to lead the way and change the status quo of our conversations. We can intentionally do that!

Who wants to be an enemy of Christ? Yet Paul is addressing believers in Philippians 3, when he says tearfully that many set their minds on earthly things, becoming enemies of Christ, and their end will be destruction (3:18–19). He gives further instruction to Timothy:

> *Be diligent to present yourself approved to God as a workman who does not need to be ashamed, accurately handling the word of truth. But avoid worldly and empty chatter, for it will lead to further ungodliness* (2 Timothy 2:15–16).

There are all levels of spiritual development in any church, and some who are not sold out to Jesus may be church members. We could find ourselves in a conversation at church with someone we assume is a believer. Quickly, by his or her emphasis on sharing details just learned about another church member, we could be led into a juicy bit of gossip. However, God may place us in just such a situation to change the conversation to pray for that talked-about person and nip the details in the bud. This is why Peter warns us to "be of sober spirit" and "be on the alert" (1 Peter 5:8).

There are many more subtle influences in our daily lives, but much like the author of Hebrews, "time will fail me" to list sensuality, sorcery, strife, jealousy, factions, and more (11:32).

CLEANSING BY THE WASHING OF THE WORD — BE CLEAN

Our prayer lives will be hindered by emphasis on worldly matters, so it is important to obey and stay alert. We need to ask, "Are the conversations I'm engaging in with other Christians edifying for our spiritual growth, or just 'worldly and empty chatter?'" (See 2 Tmothy 2:16.)

We can be proactive and intentional in our quest to become mature, clean vessels for our King's use in prayer. Bill Bright described this intentionality as *spiritual breathing*. At the moment you notice an ungodly thought or action, acknowledge it and exhale a confession to the Lord to ask for His forgiveness. Then inhale His forgiveness and a fresh filling of the Holy Spirit.

In this way, we can continually walk in righteousness with Jesus. We can stay clean by keeping short accounts with both God and man. This quick action will also prevent self-centered rationalization that our sinful thought or action was justified. Jude 24 reassures us that God is able to keep us from stumbling—we won't be functioning in our own strength but in His.

As believers, we are no longer slaves to sin,

> *Knowing this, that our old self was crucified*
> *with Him, in order that our body of sin might*
> *be done away with, so that we would no longer*
> *be slaves to sin; for he who has died is freed*
> *from sin* (Romans 6:6–7).

Sin comes when we choose our way over God's way and willfully disobey His commands.

Jesus calls us the light of the world, but like a car headlight lens can get dirty and limit the light, our lives can get dirty with unconfessed sin and render our prayers powerless, and our witness, or light, ineffective. To be clean, we need to repent and use the Scriptural soap that Jesus gives us in His Word for cleansing as described by Paul:

> *Husbands, love your wives, just as Christ also*
> *loved the church and gave Himself up for her,*
> *so that He might sanctify her,* having cleansed
> her by the washing of water with the word, *that*
> *He might present to Himself the church in all*
> *her glory, having no spot or wrinkle or any such*
> *thing; but that she would be holy and blame-*
> *less* (Ephesians 5:25–27, author's emphasis).

Using God's Word, (see Scriptural Soap in Appendix A), we can be convicted of the sins we need to confess and turn away from.

> *For the word of God is living and active and sharper than any two-edged sword, and piercing as far as the division of soul and spirit, of both joints and marrow, and able to judge the thoughts and intentions of the heart* (Hebrews 4:12).

Cleansing empowers the Holy Spirit. The writer of Hebrews says so clearly that we can have confidence to pray in Hebrews 10:22–23,

> *Having our hearts sprinkled clean from an evil conscience and our bodies washed with pure water. Let us hold fast the confession of our hope without wavering, for He who promised is faithful.*

While discussing cleansing from sin, it is important to know the difference between confession and repentance. When Jesus began His earthly ministry, He didn't say, "Confess." He said, "Repent, for the kingdom of heaven is at hand" (Matthew 4:17).

Confession is agreeing with God — often that we are wrong. Repentance means taking action to *stop* being wrong. We must change direction, take different steps, and begin new, good habits. Spend some time in prayer using the Scriptural Soap appendix (A) before beginning the next chapter about releasing the Holy Spirit's power.

Pray with Me

Father,

Forgive us for the obstacles we bring with us when we pray. We want to know Your ways so that we can know You, and be used by You in our prayers. Give us spiritual eyes to see the obstacles we are overlooking. Show us the subtle ways we offend You, our Holy God, and convict us of our sins. Pour out a spirit of repentance, so that we can turn away from these sins, be forgiven by You, and grow into the people of God You can use for Your kingdom purposes. We love You, Lord.

In Jesus' name, amen.

For Further Study

Read James 4:1–12.

• What are some obstacles to prayer listed in these verses?

• Why do we ask and not receive according to verse 3?

• What does friendship with the world cause?

• How can we get the devil to flee from us?

• What is the danger of speaking against someone?

Read James 4:17.

• What do we learn about sin in this verse?

• What is God saying to you as you meditate on it?

• Read Philippians 4:8.

• Where should we let our minds dwell?

CHAPTER THREE

UNLEASH THE POWER OF GOD IN PRAYER

"A loving spirit is a condition of believing prayer. We cannot be wrong with people and right with God."

—THE KNEELING CHRISTIAN

"Obstacles are those frightful things you see when you take your eyes off God. So don't take your eyes off the Savior. Spend less time watching the news, biting your nails, and fretting over [current events]. Spend more time in God's Word."

—MARVIN J. ROSENTHAL

"[God] is able to keep you from stumbling, and to make you stand in the presence of His glory blameless with great joy."

—JUDE 24

*W*e will find that the power that works within us is released and God works powerfully when we preserve the unity of the Spirit, pray without ceasing, consecrate ourselves, remember how great our God is, and believe that He will answer.

A right relationship with our heavenly Father paves the way for the power of the Holy Spirit to work mightily within us. Paul refers to this process as putting on the new self and describes some of the new attributes to develop, These include a "heart of compassion, kindness, humility, gentleness and patience," putting up with each other, and forgiving others (Colossians 3:12–13). "Beyond all these things put on love, which is the perfect bond of unity" (Colossians 3:14)

PRESERVE THE UNITY OF THE SPIRIT

Following Jesus is not a lone ranger endeavor. We are to teach one another, or share what God is teaching us, and hold one another accountable. Proverbs 27:17 explains, "Iron sharpens iron, so one man sharpens another." God created us to need each other and ordained that we are stronger in unity.

That is why Jesus prayed that we would be one (John 17:21). The term *Christian fellowship* not only means relationship building, but also, if not more so, means an intentional pursuit to help one another become mature, clean vessels for our King's use. We can all benefit from having an accountability partner or group. We need someone to care enough about us to ask the hard questions about our spiritual growth.

Church membership and being a part of a Bible-study group are keys to spiritual growth. God has given us gifts to serve the greater body of Christ, and we thrive in an environment of growing Christians. To develop consistency in prayer, it is helpful to join with an existing prayer group or call some friends also interested in growing in the practice of God's presence and prayer. Ask God to help you find such a group.

Jesus taught us "that if two of [us] agree on earth about anything that [we] may ask, it will be done for [us] by [our] Father who is in heaven" (Matthew 18:19). There is definite power reserved for believers who come together in unity to seek the Father's face. When Jesus taught us to pray, He used the plural, "Our Father" (Matthew 6:9). The early church is also our example of continually being devoted to prayer together.

Putting together jigsaw puzzles can be intriguing. Right out of the box, it is just a pile of disorganized pieces, and later when each piece is put together, the picture is clear. The body of Christ is a lot like a jigsaw puzzle. If we are not using our spiritual gifts for the good of the whole body we, too look disjointed. (See 1 Corinthians 12; Romans 12:3–8; and Ephesians 4:11–13 for teaching on spiritual gifts.)

God is not a God of confusion and gives spiritual gifts for the benefit of the whole body. When we bring our gifts together and use them, or fit our puzzle pieces into the whole, the picture the world sees is clear and people know we are disciples of Jesus.

Our unity and love for one another is a beautiful image of the love of Christ for others, and they cannot resist it (1 Corinthians 14:33; Ephesians 4:16; John 13:34–35; Acts 2:46–47). A church with a spirit of unity will be a church that can pray in agreement and see God work powerfully.

PRAY WITHOUT CEASING

One day when we were driving away from the house, Joel asked me if I had locked the back door. I really could not be sure I had. When we went back to check, I had locked it, but it was such a habit that I hadn't even noticed doing it.

I want my propensity to pray to be like that, a natural action. Breathing comes naturally and is essential to physical life. Praying is as essential to our spiritual lives, and with practice the inclination to pray will come just as naturally.

Steve Booth describes prayer as the life breath of the church:

> Prayer has been the life-breath of the church from its inception. From the earliest days believers have devoted themselves to prayer, individually and corporately, just as Jesus intended. In Luke's history of the expansion of the church as in his gospel, prayer plays a key role. In the pages

of Acts we discover all types of prayers—prayers of repentance, thanksgiving, rejoicing, praise and more. We see the Church praying in times of decision making and in times of crisis. We see them fasting, laying on hands, and kneeling. On occasion God spoke to his people through visions as they prayed. Both leaders and members in the early Church were committed to prayer as an indispensable part of the Christian life. Their example has challenged believers of every generation to be a people devoted to prayer. (Dan R. Crawford, compiler, *Giving Ourselves to Prayer: An Acts 6:4 Primer for Ministry,* chap. 42)

God works through the prayers of His people, so He teaches us through His Word to pray without ceasing, to be devoted to prayer, and to pray in the Spirit at all times. He gave us the indwelling Holy Spirit to equip us for His assignment. Faithful prayer—the practice of continual communion with our Holy God in good times and bad, alone or with others—is a habit we can develop, a character trait we can incorporate.

Brother Lawrence, a well-known monk, wrote a book, *The Practice of the Presence of God*, about his experience with intentionally being with God in all of the mundane work of daily life—even in dish washing. Like any habit, the more you practice prayer, the more prayer becomes a way of life.

Recently, at a Bible study on Romans 12:1–2, Stuart Milne, another Bible-study teacher, closed the study in prayer. Before he prayed, he shared a related experience he and his wife had on vacation when they visited the Oregon Trail in western Nebraska. They saw the hill where settlers had to drive their wagons, and they saw the deep ruts in the ground still visible from the wagons repeatedly going on the same path and settling into the same ruts made back in 1849–50. Over time the ruts seemed petrified.

Stuart said seeing the ruts reminded him of bad habits that can become so ingrained in our brains that they are difficult to remove. However, even the worst habits can be transformed by the renewing of our minds and replaced by good habits. I thought this was a good analogy of how ingrained habits of any kind can become.

The command to renew our minds is the key (Romans 12:2). Developing good prayer practices will take perseverance but can become like the highways to Zion in our hearts that bless us with strength in God (Psalm 84:5). These would be good ruts, well-worn paths to the Lord!

There may be times in our discipline of the spiritual walk when prayer seems dry or ineffective, but especially in those times of testing, we must remain faithful. We may pray with the psalmist, "O God, You are my God; I shall seek You earnestly; my soul thirsts for You, my flesh yearns for You, in a dry and weary land where there is no water" (Psalm 63:1).

The Bible shows us that the prophet Daniel had a dry experience that could have caused him to give up, but he remained faithful by fasting and weeping in prayer for three weeks. He was blessed by a visit from an angel and their conversation gives us insight into the heavenly battle being fought as we pray.

> *Then [the angel of the Lord] said to me, "Do not be afraid, Daniel, for from the first day that you set your heart on understanding this and on humbling yourself before your God, your words were heard, and I have come in response to your words. But the prince of the kingdom of Persia was withstanding me for twenty-one days; then behold, Michael, one of the chief princes, came to help me, for I had been left there with the kings of Persia* (Daniel 10:12–13).

We may not have an angel visit to commend us like Daniel did, but we can know that God notices when we are faithful, and He works powerfully. There is a battle in the heavenly places and our prayers give fuel to the fight. God acts on behalf of the one who waits or perseveres in prayer (Isaiah 64:4).

Remember the story about demon removal in which Jesus taught His disciples "This kind cannot come out by anything but prayer" (Mark 9:21–29)? God has ordained that there are things He will not do except in response to prayer. A Puritan put it this way, "The prayers of the saints are the beginning of the execution of the predetermined purposes of God."

E. M. Bounds agreed in *The Weapon of Prayer*, "Praying saints are God's agents for carrying on His saving and providential work on earth . . . Praying agents of the Most High are always forerunners of spiritual prosperity." God said, "This also I will let the house of Israel ask Me to do for them" (Ezekiel 36:37). Our prayers are important to God.

Beatrice, the woman I mentioned in the previous chapter, who was struggling to find time to pray, met with a more mature believer to discuss her hindrance. This caring lady suggested Beatrice use the times with her children to teach them to pray, too, so they would better understand what she was doing when they found her kneeling by her bed with head bowed. Beatrice began to pray aloud about situations or people they encountered as she took the children on errands. She discovered budding intercessors before her eyes.

Her children, Paul and Janie, began to suggest things to pray about and became her accountability prompters on prayerwalks and drives. For example, in response to the news of forest fires and the firemen who were battling the flames, they had been praying for firemen. Then one day when they were driving, a fire truck with sirens blaring passed by them. Janie cried out, "Mommy, we need to pray!"

Children often understand prayer and trusting God easier than some adults. Prayer became a natural part and the first option in their family instead of the last resort. Praying for their daddy kept him close in their hearts and minds and made the transition to his return go smoother. They had trusted God to protect him and thanked God for their husband and daddy being home again.

Enlisting a prayer partner to pray with us gives us mutual accountability and is a good way to pray continually and "to stimulate one another to love and good deeds . . . encouraging one another" (Hebrews 10:24–25). Do you have a prayer partner?

BE CONSECRATED FOR GOD'S USE

To be consecrated for our Master's use, He must be everything to us. While costly, the eternal value of being consecrated is worth so much more than anything we give up. Jesus will give us all the strength we need to consecrate ourselves because it is God who sanctifies us (Philippians 4:13; Leviticus 20:7–8).

It is countercultural, few aspire to it and even fewer live this way. However, if we want to mature in Christ, honor God, and be used by Him in our prayers, we must stay on the narrow road (Matthew 7:13–14). We see how narrow the way is when Jesus tells us that we cannot serve two masters (Matthew 6:24).

Peter said in his first letter: "Like the Holy One who called you, be holy yourselves also in all your behavior; because it is written, 'YOU SHALL BE HOLY, FOR I AM HOLY'" (1 Peter 1:14–16). How does this play out in current events?

Televisions are found just about everywhere in the public arena, so when a Christian family went into a fast food restaurant to eat, they were confronted with a vulgar sitcom they did not want their family to watch. The dad quickly went to the TV and changed the station.

I heard this story because another Christian couple we know was also eating there and said they suddenly felt convicted. They had been blithely watching the show and laughing at the coarse jokes. We live in a secular world where we are continually exposed to worldly values. To stay consecrated, we need to be alert and take any action we can. When one Christian takes a stand, suddenly other Christians are influenced to stick to their values too.

One Christian can encourage another in many ways. Joel and I usually tell our restaurant waiter or waitress that we are going to thank God for our food and ask if there is any way we can pray for them. Usually there is a positive response—they want a tip, after all—but often it leads to a spiritual conversation.

One day, when we offered to pray for our waitress, her face lit up and she said, "Yes, and I will pray with you!" After we prayed for her, she told us she had been asking God to give her opportunities to pray for people in the dining room where she worked, and we were an answer to her prayers. Another couple commented as they left that they were so glad to see us pray with our waitress. There are Christians all around.

The body of Christ working together in unity can help each other stay consecrated to God by encouraging one another to be bold in our faith and courageous in our public actions. I have been encouraged by how many people I see bowing to thank God for their food in public places. There is also an increase in Bibles being read in public places. We need not be ashamed of the gospel or of the spiritual disciplines we employ, even in public.

God desires for us to be and stay clean for His name's sake, and He knows our hearts (Isaiah 43:25). If we want to stay clean before Him, we can ask God to keep us back from "presumptuous sins" or "hidden faults" that could hinder our prayers, like David did in Psalm 19:12–13.

REMEMBER WHAT GOD HAS SAID AND DONE

Another good way to consecrate ourselves for God's use is to remember God, both what He has said and done. Psalm 105:5 says, "Remember His wonders which He has done, His marvels and the judgments uttered by His mouth." Asaph and his brothers went a step further in the celebration upon the return of the ark, and said to not only remember but also "make known His deeds among the peoples" (1 Chronicles 16:8).

One time when the subject being taught was "remembering," I asked the group to share their favorite Bible story. Responses were slow in coming. One mentioned David and Goliath, and another said Joseph and his coat of many colors. So I began to ask if they remembered specific examples such as Daniel and the lion's den or Moses with the burning bush. (See Psalms 77:11; 105:5; 111:1–4; and 143:5 about remembering.) Once their memories had been jogged and with Bibles in hand, many more Bible characters were shouted out.

An animated discussion arose with group suggestions that we should talk about these mighty deeds of God with our children. Instead of making sure they know all the nursery rhymes, we should teach children Bible stories, poetry from Psalms, and wisdom from Proverbs. Many Psalms encourage relating stories about God's mighty deeds to the next generation and talking about them as families. (see 78:4–7; 89:1; 96:3, 7; 102:18; and 103:17–18).

We are to love God so much that we keep His words in our hearts and teach them to our children and grandchildren. God speaks:

> *These words, which I am commanding you today, shall be on your heart. You shall teach them diligently to your sons and shall talk of them when you sit in your house and when you walk by the way and when you lie down and when you rise up* (Deuteronomy 6:6–8).

Imagine the transformation we could see in just one or two generations if Christian families obediently spent time in God's

Word together and became conversant about how great our God is. As we repeat stories about the mighty deeds He has done for and through His people since creation, we grow in our faith and trust Him more easily with everything. Another benefit of remembering and focusing on God's faithfulness in the past is renewal of our minds (Romans 12:2).

No doubt it makes a difference in the way we pray when we have a steady reserve of memories of the ways God has been faithful and is in control. A prayer journal is a great tool to support our memory reserve, by our recording those times when God shows us something new in His Word or when we see Him at work. While it is protective to remember His deeds, it is strategically important that we remember His commands and obey them. Obedience is the way we show our love for God (John 14:15, 21).

God told Moses to have the children of Israel make tassels on the corners of their garments throughout their generations and to put a blue cord or ribbon on each tassel. He explained:

> It shall be a tassel for you to look at and remember all the commandments of the LORD, so as to do them and not follow after your own heart and your own eyes . . . so that you may remember to do all My commandments and be holy to your God. I am the LORD your God (Numbers 15:39–41).

Remembering requires Scripture memory so that the Holy Spirit can bring to our minds what we have "programmed" into our computer-like brains. God's Word convicts, cleanses, and protects us from sin, gives guidance as a lamp to our feet and a light to our paths. When we trust in the Lord with all our hearts, lean not on our own understanding, and acknowledge Him in all our ways, He will make our paths straight (Psalm 119:11; 105; Proverbs 3:5–6).

An elder and Bible teacher at Johnson Ferry Baptist Church in Atlanta, Georgia, John Farish said it this way. "Obedience can only come with knowledge of God's commands, so memorize and meditate on Scripture—bake it into your life."

GROW IN BELIEF

The story of King Jehoshaphat is a great example of how to handle the crises that arise in our lives through remembering what God has done in the past, and believing He will handle the current crisis. When King Jehoshaphat received word that three vast armies had joined forces to make war against him, he "was afraid and turned his attention to seek the LORD" (2 Chronicles 20:3).

He proclaimed a fast throughout Judah, and all the people, including women and children, came from all the cities to seek the Lord together. He began his prayer by praising God, proclaiming before all the people how great and all-powerful God is.

He listed some of His past accomplishments on behalf of Abraham's descendants. Finally Jehoshaphat declared, "We are powerless before this great multitude who are coming against us; nor do we know what to do, but our eyes are on You" (20:12) God answered exceeding, abundantly beyond what Jehoshaphat could have imagined. God spoke through one of the priests and proclaimed, "Do not fear or be dismayed because of this great multitude, for the battle is not yours but God's" (20:15).

They still had to go out to the battlefield the next day, but in one accord the king and his people bowed down and worshipped the Lord. They believed God would do what He said He would do before He did it.

God's delivery was amazing and miraculous. Jehoshaphat gave the people an encouraging word to put their trust in the Lord, then "he appointed those who sang to the Lord and those who praised Him in holy attire" to go out before the army (20:21).

God's timing is perfect. "*When* they began singing and praising, the Lord set ambushes against the sons of Ammon, Moab and Mount Seir, who had come against Judah; so they were routed" (20:22, author's emphasis). God saw to it that the three armies destroyed each other and left enough valuable "spoil" that it took the people three days to collect it all. But on the fourth day, they assembled to bless the Lord and then returned "to Jerusalem with joy for the Lord had made them to rejoice over their enemies" (20:27).

Jehoshaphat and his people believed God would do what He said He would do, and their belief was the key to God releasing His power on their behalf. Jesus taught this principle when He said, "And all things you ask in prayer, believing, you will receive" (Matthew 21:22).

Jesus gave examples of how our believing faith contributes to answered prayer in His ministry. There was a woman who had been suffering from a hemorrhage and thought, "If I only touch His garment, I shall get well" (Matthew 9:21). Jesus turned and saw her and said, "Daughter, take courage; your faith has made you well" (9:22).

Then later, as some blind men followed Him, He turned and asked, "'Do you believe that I am able to do this?' They said to Him, 'Yes, Lord.' Then He touched their eyes saying, 'It shall be done to you according to your faith.' And their eyes were opened" (9:28–30).

Hebrews 11:6 is a verse to memorize: "And without faith it is impossible to please Him, for he who comes to God must believe that He is, and that He is a rewarder of those who seek Him."

There is a reason followers of Jesus are called *believers:* our work is to believe. After Jesus multiplied the bread and fed the thousands, a multitude started to follow Him. John records the interaction between Jesus and the crowd. "Therefore they said to Him, 'What shall we do, so that we may work the works of God?' Jesus answered and said to them, 'This is the work of God, that you believe in Him whom He has sent'" (John 6:28–29).

In summary, the power that works within us is released and God works when we preserve the unity of the Spirit, pray without ceasing, consecrate ourselves, remember how great our God is, and believe that He will answer.

Father,

Thank You for clothing us with Your righteousness by the power of the shed blood of Jesus. Help us to preserve the unity of the Spirit in the bond of peace. Intensify our awareness of Your presence in our daily lives so we pray about everything. Help us to be consecrated to You alone for Your sake and for Your good pleasure. Father, keep us in Your name and Your Word as Jesus prayed for us in John 17. Lord, You tell us repeatedly in Your Word to remember You and Your mighty deeds because memory is our protection from the sins that could so easily entangle us. Empower us to grow in our belief that You are who You say You are, and will do what You have promised. Increase our faith Lord, we pray.

In Jesus' name, amen.

For Further Study

Read John 14:13–15.

• Why does Jesus answer prayers we ask in His name?

• What is the way we show our love for Jesus?

Read 1 Chronicles 14:8–17.

• What did David do when the Philistines made a raid against him?

• How does God show that He values obedience?

• Read 1 John 5:14–15.

• What gives us confidence in prayer?

• Can we know that God will answer our prayer?

CHAPTER FOUR

MATURITY IN PRAYER GLORIFIES GOD

"History belongs to the intercessors who believe the future into being."

—WALTER WINK, *THE POWERS THAT BE*

"It comes the very moment you wake up each morning. All your wishes and hopes for the day rush at you like wild animals. And the first job each morning consists simply in shoving them all back; in listening to that other voice, taking that other point of view, letting that other, larger, stronger, quieter life [of God] come flowing in."

—C. S. LEWIS, *MERE CHRISTIANITY*

"But thanks be to God, who gives us the victory through our Lord Jesus Christ."

—I CORINTHIANS 15:57

Our spiritual maturity in prayer gives glory to God by our love for Him and our focus on Him and what He is doing. With our focus more steadily on Him and His purposes, we can pray as Jesus taught us, "Your will be done, on earth as it is in heaven" (Matthew 6:10). Our praying on earth is also spiritual preparation for our reigning with Jesus in eternity.

TRAINING FOR REIGNING

It is amazing to realize the future plans God has for us because we are His children. He says in Revelation 20:6,

> *Blessed and holy is the one who has a part in the first resurrection; over these the second death has no power, but they will be priests of God and of Christ and will reign with Him for a thousand years.*

Jesus said to His disciples, "But the one who endures to the end, he will be saved" (Matthew 24:13). Paul confirms this in his second letter to Timothy, "If we endure, we will also reign with Him" (2 Timothy 2:12). *Endure* is a short, easy-to-pronounce word, but its meaning and the living it out are challenging, to say the least.

Enduring involves knowledge of Scripture, obedience, perseverance, and faithfulness to the end of our lives. Jesus says that he who overcomes will be invited to sit with Him on His throne. We may have tribulation in the meantime, but Jesus has overcome the world and teaches us to overcome evil with good (Revelation 3:21; John 16:33; Romans 12:21).

Paul wrote about this when he counseled the early believers in Corinth to settle their differences with each other rather than take any disagreements to a secular court (1 Corinthians 6:1–7). He reminded them that we will judge angels in the future, so how much more are we able to judge matters of this life?

John adds to our understanding by explaining that our faith in God and being born of Him gives us the victory needed to overcome, and thereby reign with Jesus, because we believe that Jesus is the Son of God (1 John 5:4–5; cf. 2 Timothy 2:12).

The heavenly reward is worth being overcomers here on earth. Overcoming includes practicing our faith and belief in Jesus to build them up, like spiritual muscle. We can endure to the end in joy by taking it one day at a time empowered by the Holy Spirit. Jesus tells us in Revelation 21:7, "He who overcomes will inherit these things, and I will be his God and he will be My son."

In summary, a goal of prayer is maturity because God is training us to reign with Him in eternity. He equips us through our experience of regularly spending time with Him in His Word and in His throne room. The psalmist reveals, "You will make known to me the path of life; in Your presence is fullness of joy; [i]n Your right hand there are pleasures forever" (Psalm 16:11).

STEPS TO MATURITY IN PRAYER

New believers start out like newborn babies, spiritually, and some remain at that level without discipleship. However, we are taught to grow up into mature followers of Christ. Those who only listen to others preach or teach the Word and never study it for themselves are still being spoon-fed like infants.

To mature, we must become self-feeders, learning how to accurately understand and share with others the meat, or truth, of God's Word. At each stage of growth, we learn more about Jesus, until we truly know Him in a joyful, loving relationship. Scriptures that speak to the need for us to mature in our faith include 1 Corinthians 3:1–3; Ephesians 4:11–16; and Hebrews 5:11–14.

There is much that God wants to teach us and that takes time. Jesus told His disciples, "I have many more things to say to you, but you cannot bear them now" (John 16:12). The advantage we have on this side of the Cross is that the Holy Spirit reveals truth to us as we read God's Word.

The following five action steps can help us move victoriously toward maturity in prayer that glorifies God.

DIE TO SELF

Jesus was teaching His disciples what it takes to follow Him when He said:

And He was saying to them all, "If anyone wishes to come after Me, he must deny himself, and take up his cross daily and follow Me. For whoever wishes to save his life will lose it, but whoever loses his life for My sake, he is the one who will save it (Luke 9:23–24).

To die to self is to lose every vestige of pride and self-importance, to take off the spiritual-giant mask that church members (and spiritual leaders) so often wear to impress each other. Francis Frangipane said it well, "Jesus meets us on the way to 'demask us.'" We need to be real to be Christ like. To grow in maturity, we must die to self — daily.

Paul explains to the Galatians,

I have been crucified with Christ; and it is no longer I who live, but Christ lives in me; and the life which I now live in the flesh I live by faith in the Son of God, who loved me and gave Himself up for me (Galatians 2:20).

When we understand and agree that we are no longer our own, we become vessels God will use for His purposes and glory. We were bought with an incredibly high price and we belong to Jesus. We are of great value to our Father.

God is described frequently as the potter and we as His clay, "All of us are the work of [His] hand" (Isaiah 64:8). Sometimes our potter may break us so that He can remake us into something better. The psalmist was quite familiar with brokenness both in heart and spirit (Psalms 34:18, 51:17, et al.). An old hymn by Adelaide A. Pollard sums up our attitude in dying to self: "Have Thine own way, Lord! Have Thine own way! Thou art the Potter, I am the clay. Mold me and make me after Thy will, while I am waiting, yielded and still." May our desire to mature in prayer lead us to die to self and humbly surrender to God's purposes.

LISTEN TO GOD AND FOLLOW JESUS

Seeing ourselves as apprentices, learning from God, will help us listen more and obey rather than coming to the place of prayer with a self-focused agenda. With practice, we will be able to recognize our Good Shepherd's voice and follow Him as Jesus described (John 10:4, 27).

One good way to hear God is to ask Him to speak and reveal truth from His Word as we read. When He stops us, we need to meditate, reread, and just be still while thinking about what He is saying. Ask questions including the what, who, why, where, and how. *Is there a promise I need to pray? Is there a command I am disobeying? Do I need to confess sin?*

What are the important points of the verse where God stopped me? What is the context? Let Scripture interpret

Scripture by cross-referencing and reading other translations of the same passage. As it marinates in our minds all day, the points highlighted may be instructive, encouraging, convicting, or restorative.

Jesus is the leader. As His followers, we must fix our eyes on Him and follow Him closely (Hebrews 12:2). We are also told to be "imitators of God, as beloved children" and to "walk as children of Light" bearing the Light's fruit of goodness, righteousness, and truth, trying to learn what is pleasing to the Lord (Ephesians 5:1, 8–10).

Jesus often said, "He who has ears to hear, let him hear" (Matthew 11:15).Listening and following Jesus go hand in hand, just as listening and obeying bring joy to our Father's heart. God primarily speaks through His Word, both as we read and when He brings verses or passages to our minds at appropriate times of need.

Sometimes God will speak through His Word, through other people, and through our circumstances, all in harmony. The more we learn to listen, the more we hear Him also speak into our minds. The following is a trivial example, but demonstrates that God cares about the small details of our lives as well as the big, life-impacting things.

One day I had gone home for lunch and when I was ready to go back to the church where I worked, I could not find my car keys. After I looked a minute, I prayed and said, "God You know I need to go back to work where I am serving You, and I know that nothing is lost from You. Will You show me where my keys are?"

A thought immediately popped into my mind, "Look on the hearth of the fireplace." I had never put my keys there and would probably never have looked there. But there they were! I believed that if I asked Him, God would answer.

The more we mature in our prayer lives, the more we will just as automatically ask Him in believing faith for healing; protection; provision; or salvation for friends, family, cities, and the nations and believe that He will answer. That is the victory God wants to give us in prayer.

God demonstrated through His Word that He is patient and understanding when we need a "fleece" of assurance. The story of Gideon is an example of lively interaction with God. Gideon was honest, fearful, incredulous of the calling, and had doubts. It is also a great example of the way God sees us.

The Lord called Gideon a "valiant warrior" and so Gideon became one (Judges 6:12ff). Their dialogue shows the patience and the lengths God will go to, to help us be sure we are hearing Him. God does not call the equipped, but just as He did for Gideon, He equips those whom He calls. We need to be listening.

Lingering to listen to God becomes our most treasured occupation when we grasp that nothing compares with Him. Finding His wisdom and gaining understanding are more profitable than silver or gold, and more precious than jewels (Psalm 84:10; Proverbs 3:13–15). Gaining wisdom and understanding also makes it easier to turn loose of anything that distracts us from Him.

God knows our hearts, wants to transform our hearts, and is looking for men and women with hearts after His own heart— like David—those He can trust to hear Him and obey. That makes it worth spending focused, uninterrupted times alone with God, just being still and listening.

God will teach us to hear His voice if we are interested. We will find Him when we search for Him with all our hearts (Jeremiah 29:12–13). One day at a time, interaction with our Father can be life changing and eternity impacting. God will reveal more and more of Himself and His purposes as He sees in us a heart of worship, of devotion, and of willingness to listen to God and follow Jesus.

Turn Loose the Controls

A great benefit of following Jesus is that He teaches us not to worry about anything but to trust Him completely in every situation. In the Sermon on the Mount, He asks a very logical question, "And who of you by being worried can add a single hour to his life?" (Matthew 6:27). When we try to control situations, we tend to mess things up because of our limited knowledge of the big picture.

My daddy used to tell me that he believed I would worry if I didn't have something to worry about. Teaching me to trust Jesus, he helped me memorize a wonderful promise about worry or anxiety.

Be anxious for nothing, but in everything by prayer and supplication with thanksgiving let your requests be made known to God. And the peace of God, which surpasses all comprehension, will guard your hearts and your minds in Christ Jesus (Philippians 4:6–7).

I love the peace that passes all understanding but sometimes I still have to confess to God that I have slipped into anxiety. I want to be obedient and give my concern to Him in prayer. Praising God through the alphabet after I tell Him my concern takes my mind off of that concern (See my previously published book, *Prayer 101*). Basically, when I turn my eyes and attention to Jesus, the concern that caused me anxiety settles back into perspective. It is very small in comparison to my huge God. Once again I can enjoy His peace.

When we agree to give up the pride of life and our "right" to be right along with the other sins we discussed in chapter two, then we can sing an old hymn as an act of worship, "I Surrender All" to the lordship of our King. We were bought with a price and are no longer our own. The burden goes away, too, when we release control. We gain freedom in Christ.

Peter gives further instruction for turning loose the control of our lives in his first letter, saying, "Therefore humble yourselves under the mighty hand of God, that He may exalt you at the proper time, casting all your anxiety on Him, because He cares for you" (1 Peter 5:6–7). Why would we want to carry around a lot of stress and anxiety when we can trust our Lord to lead us in the way we should go? Besides, being connected to Jesus is the way to accomplish things of eternal significance.

Jesus clarifies our fruit-bearing potential when He uses the analogy of the vine and branches (John 15:1–11). He says that apart from Him we can do nothing but promises that if we abide in Him, we *will* bear fruit (15:5). He then tells us that we bring glory to God when we bear fruit and prove to be His disciples (15:8). He reminds us that obedience is the key to abiding in Him, and He encourages us that when we abide in and trust Him, we will abide in His love (15:10). Finally we get to see the motive for Jesus teaching us these vineyard truths: "These things I have spoken to you so that My joy may be in you, and that your joy may be made full" (15:11). The joy of the Lord is our strength and His ways are so much better than ours. Instead of worry, let's turn loose the controls and give them to Jesus.

Grow Spiritually

There is discipline involved in our spiritual growth, but, like most discipline, it is rewarding. Building a love relationship with God is actually a great joy. The more we read and study the Bible the more we get to know God, His commands, and His promises.

Second Timothy 2:15 is a good memory verse. "Be diligent to present yourself approved to God as a workman who does not need to be ashamed, accurately handling the word of truth."

Our son, Joel, and I were talking about how God gives promises He intends to fulfill when he shared an experience that illustrates this fact. He had been praying that his Navigator campus ministry would be like Zechariah 8:23—he wanted it to be evident that he was walking with God, that others would "grasp [his] garment" and say, "Let us go with you, for we have heard that God is with you."

When he was trying to find Jim, a new believer he was mentoring, he saw Jim's car and grabbed a picnic table nearby to wait for him to return. He had his Bible, so he took advantage of the time. It was Monday night around ten. Within a few minutes two guys came walking up. Joel recognized one of them and knew they were unbelievers. They stopped and asked what he was doing. He replied, "I'm reading the Bible." One said, "Well, we don't have anything to do, can we join you?" After going through some of the Book of Matthew, Joel invited them to NavNight that Thursday. The one he knew better came and gave his life to Christ.

Meanwhile, Joel's roommate, Josh, wanted to take a road trip to another campus to administer surveys so he could see where that campus was spiritually. They decided to go after the NavNight. A guy named Nick asked if he could tag along saying, "I wanted to see what you guys do." On Sunday, a high school student, Alec, grabbed Joel saying, "I'd love to meet with you and learn from you." That was when Joel realized that God had been fulfilling Zechariah 8:23 right before his eyes! God wants us to pray His promises and see His kingdom expand.

Reading the Bible in public often generates interest as in Joel's story. I took a multiflight trip near the first of the year, and as I was reading through the Bible again, I was in Leviticus. On the first leg, a man sat down and asked if I was enjoying Leviticus. I laughed and said, "Yes, I'm plowing through." He was a believer, and we exchanged encouraging words.

On the next leg, a lady sat next to me across the aisle from her husband and son. She was talking with them a while, then she commented to me that I looked like I was enjoying reading the Bible. I showed her the surprisingly exciting verses I was reading. It was Leviticus 9:23–24, about the glory of the Lord appearing to the people, fire consuming the burnt offering, and the people shouting and falling on their faces. She agreed that it did sound exciting.

I learned that the woman had been a church attender at one time but had not been to church in more than six months. She turned to talk with her husband, and I moved to the Book of Acts to review what I would be teaching when I arrived in Springfield.

She turned back to me and leaned in to see what I was reading now and asked, "What else exciting are you reading?" Our conversation soon got serious about her spiritual condition and her beliefs about God. By the end of the flight, she was talking about reading her Bible again because she, too, wanted to follow

Jesus. God's Word really does not return void (Isaiah 55:11).

Knowing for ourselves the truth of God's Word, the good, helps us recognize evil and lies. Jesus describes the devil as "a liar, and the father of lies" (John 8:44). Remember the way he tempted Jesus in the wilderness? The devil loves to take Scripture out of context with his lies. (see Luke 4:9–12).

John gives us a way to discern good from evil when he writes, "Beloved, do not believe every spirit, but test the spirits to see whether they are from God, because many false prophets have gone out into the world" (1 John 4:1).

With warnings like this, we may wonder how we can keep our way pure. Thankfully Psalm 119 gives us many supporting benefits of studying the precepts, commandments, ordinances, statutes, and testimonies of Scripture. It even gives important reasons for memorizing Scripture, "Your word I have treasured in my heart, [t]hat I may not sin against You" (Psalm 119:11). Growing in the knowledge of God's Word transforms us by renewing our minds, so that we can know the will of God (Romans 12:1–2).

I remember one day on my drive to the North American Mission Board offices, a car cut in front of me, and I had to slow down. Suddenly, I noticed the daffodils that were blooming next to the road, and I gave an automatic praise to God for their beauty. Then I started laughing out loud and prayed, "Lord, that was You! You are working in my life."

I could remember my former reaction to such an intrusion that was far different in years past. It was frustration and impatience back then, not notice of beauty. God does refine and polish us as we spend time with Him seeking to grow in our spiritual lives. The motto for the women's college I attended was, "That our daughters may be as corner stones, polished after the similitude of a palace" (Psalm 144:12, KJV).

BECOME MORE LIKE JESUS

We become more and more like that which we worship, so the more we focus on and worship our living Lord Jesus, the more we will become like Him. Jesus pointed us to His Father, and our role is to point people to Jesus (John 5:19, 14:10, 15:5). Paul describes God's plan for us in his letter to the Romans, "For those whom He foreknew, He also predestined to become conformed to the image of His Son, so that He would be the first-born among many brethren" (Romans 8:29).

Jesus doesn't whitewash the suffering we might endure. He instructs us to fear not those who kill the body, but fear God who is able to destroy both soul and body in hell (Matthew 10:28). It is a sobering reminder of what becoming like Jesus may involve. Jesus goes on to encourage and remind us, though, how very valuable we are to God (10:29–31).

This is not an exhaustive list of ways to grow into maturity but will certainly point us in the right direction. The Holy Spirit is our Teacher who will bring us into all truth and reveal things from our Father in heaven. Paul gives us hope for our objective of spiritual maturity in his first letter to the Corinthians:

> *When the perfect comes, the partial will be done away. When I was a child, I used to speak like a child, think like a child, reason like a child; when I became a man, I did away with childish things. For now we see in a mirror dimly, but then face to face; now I know in part, but then I will know fully just as I also have been fully known* (1 Corinthians 13:10–12).

We can hold on to that promise.

GIVE GOD THE GLORY IN PRAYER

A huge step toward maturity in our walk with our Lord will be ours when we desire for our prayers to bring God glory. Being interested in what is on the heart of God and doing what He initiates will bring glory to God. Isaiah clarifies that God created us for His glory and He says about Himself, "I am the LORD, that is My name; I will not give My glory to another" (Isaiah 42:8; see 43:7).

We need to "let [our] light[s] shine before men in such a way that they may see [our] good works and glorify [our] Father who is in heaven" (Matthew 5:16). The more we understand God's ways, the more we will know Him and grow in boldness, exercise believing prayer, and bring glory to Him.

Jesus gave us a tremendous prayer promise with a condition in John 14:13–15: "Whatever you ask in My name, that will I do, so that the Father may be glorified in the Son. If you ask Me anything in My name, I will do it. If you love Me, you will keep My commandments." When we obey Him and seek our Father's glory, He is the One who prompts our prayers so they line up with God's will. May that be our objective in prayer.

Review the list below and add other points you found in this chapter.

If we endure, we will reign with Jesus. The following five steps help us mature in our faith and prayers:
• Die to self
• Listen to God and follow Jesus
• Turn loose the controls
• Grow spiritually
• Become more like Jesus
Jesus answers our prayers to bring glory to God.

These are steps we can take to grow in the spiritual disciplines, but Jesus prayed that God our Father would sanctify us in His truth, which is His Word (John 17:17). "It is God who is at work in you, both to will and to work for His good pleasure" (Philippians 2:13). We are not alone when we pray. Both Jesus and the Holy Spirit are interceding for us right now (Romans 8:26, 34).

Pray with Me

Father,

Thank You for the future You have planned for us for eternity. We confess that we don't feel ready to reign with You on Your throne in heaven. Lord, thank You, though, *for equipping us with the Holy Spirit for every good work you give us to do. Help us to listen, be obedient to You, and to seek Your glory in everything we do. Help us to grow into maturity in Christ and to be overcomers.*

In Jesus' name, amen.

For Further Study

Read Psalm 84.

• What phrases indicate an intense desire to live in God's presence?

• What does God give to those who walk uprightly, in verse 11?

• How would you sum up the chapter and can you relate to it?

Read Isaiah 43:7.

• What do you learn about those called by God's name?

• Why were we created?

Read Isaiah 48:9–11.

• Whose name is God protecting by delaying His wrath?

• How did He test the children of Israel?

• What does God say about His glory?

CHAPTER FIVE

WORKING WITH GOD
THROUGH PRAYER

"He could have bestowed these things on us even without prayers; but He wished that by our prayers we should be taught from Whom these benefits come."

—ST. AUGUSTINE

"O Lord, I am yours. Do what seems good in your sight, and give me complete resignation to Your will."

—DAVID LIVINGSTON

"Whether we think of, or speak to, God, whether we act or suffer for Him, all is prayer, when we have no other object than His love, and the desire of pleasing Him. All that a Christian does, even in eating and sleeping, is prayer, when it is done in simplicity, according to the order of God . . . In souls filled with love, the desire to please God is a continual prayer."

—JOHN WESLEY

"For we are His workmanship, created in Christ Jesus for good works, which God prepared beforehand so that we would walk in them."

—EPHESIANS 2:10

*W*ork is not a curse. God gave Adam meaningful work to do before he and Eve sinned. There is purpose in our lives when we have meaningful work to do. God created us that way and gives us assignments that impact eternity. Working with God involves conversation or interaction.

When our children were young and playing at my feet, our relationship was different than it is now; they have grown up and have families of their own. Our conversations are deeper and richer. I love to hear what they think and often learn new insights from them.

By examining the Scripture, we find evidence that God our Father has a longing to engage us, His children, in rich conversation. He greatly desires for us to listen to Him, and He will hear our concerns, questions, and insecurities without judgment. I think of Moses, Joshua, and Gideon and their insecurities that God developed into strength because they trusted Him and obeyed.

It is obvious that David, a man after God's own heart, held nothing back in his conversations with God (see 1 Samuel 13:14). We, too, can be ourselves knowing that we are loved beyond description both when we are on top of the world and when we are in the pits emotionally.

God invites us to call on Him and He will answer and tell us "great and mighty things" that we do not know (Jeremiah 33:3). Our meaningful conversation is birthed out of an intimate relationship built over time spent together.

GOD'S FELLOW WORKERS

A familiar story tells of a little boy on his daddy's shoulders picking apples. When they come in, he brags to his mom about all the apples *he* picked. Like him, we may think we should get the credit for any harvest, but as more mature believers, we know that we're equipped to gather the fruit only because God our Father is lifting us up on His shoulder to let us reach it. He delights to have us on His team, though, and will give us opportunities to be in the right place at the right time.

Prayer is far more important to God than it is to us because He created this wireless connection with His children, and He knows the power of it. He invites us to work alongside Him to accomplish His purposes. He has given His promises in His Word for us to pray them into being. We are to call out to Him day and night and give Him no rest until He completes what He has said He will do. (See Isaiah 62:6–7; Ezekiel 36:37; Luke 11:5–10; 18:1.) Pray that God will call out a remnant that will do just that.

God can see the big picture and knows when and where there is a battle in the heavenly places, for which He wants our prayers to fuel the victory. The deeper our relationship and the more trust our Father has in us to be faithful to pray, the more often we will be given eternity-impacting work to do.

An important point we need to understand is that we may be on God's winning team, but there is only one star. Paul clarified this to the early church members at Corinth to correct their allegiance from one of God's fellow workers to God Himself:

> *What then is Apollos? And what is Paul? Servants through whom you believed, even as the Lord gave opportunity to each one. I planted, Apollos watered, but God was causing the growth. So then neither the one who plants nor the one who waters is anything, but God who causes the growth* (1 Corinthians 3:5–7).

We work with God, but He gets the glory.

God declares His position on this when He says, "I am the LORD, that is My name; I will not give My glory to another" (Isaiah 42:8). As fellow workers with Christ, we must be alert and quickly deflect any adoration or glory given to us to God.

We learn how to do this by the example of Peter (Acts 3:16). He quickly gave the credit to God for the miraculous healing of the man lame from birth. We, too, must be quick to give the credit to God for any blessing someone attributes to us or for any good work we do. It is all about Him.

Jesus gave us insight into the way He worked with His Father by telling the disciples He could do nothing unless it was something He saw His Father doing (John 5:19). He then said that He could do nothing of His own initiative (5:30). Jesus gave the basis for His actions when He said, "I do not seek My own will, but the will of Him who sent Me."

Our eternal King was content to be a fellow worker on earth with God the Father in heaven. He explains further that He will answer our prayers in His name, to empower our work with Him, so that the Father may be glorified in the Son (John 14:13). What a promise! What a winning system. Fellow workers can avoid pride and all its pitfalls.

GOD DESIRES FOR NONE TO PERISH

Before we can accomplish anything in our work or on a team, we need to know what an employer's or team leader's objective is for our assignment. What do they want us to accomplish? When we work with God, we don't have to wonder about that. God says throughout His Word that His objective is to save sinners, to rescue the perishing, and reclaim mankind that He created from the captivity of darkness. He desires for none to perish.

In his second letter, we are assured by Peter that, "The Lord is not slow about His promise, as some count slowness, but is patient toward you, not wishing for any to perish but for all to come to repentance" (2 Peter 3:9). Since we know God's desire for all to come to know Him, we can pray in confidence for anyone He puts on our minds and hearts.

Salvation isn't just for special people. Jesus said "whoever," and that includes even the most unlikely to follow Jesus. We must spread the good news generously and leave the results to God. I met Helen, a friend of mine, at the airport back when one could meet an incoming passenger at the gate, and was convicted by her habitual action.

Between the arrival gate and baggage claim, we stopped at a newsstand and as she paid, she asked the cashier in a friendly, lighthearted fashion, "Do you know Jesus?" The cashier smiled and said she wasn't sure, so Helen proceeded to tell her how she could know for sure. It was obvious to me this was a way of life for Helen.

She ended our conversation with the very interested cashier by saying, "We better get ready, 'cause Jesus is coming soon!" Her attitude and *glow* of lingering with Jesus gave her engaging manner success in nurturing the seed already planted in the cashier's life. Helen engaged three more people before we even left the airport.

THE BATTLE FOR SOULS
IS WON ON OUR KNEES

The whole redemption process begins, is fueled by, and ends with prayer—interaction with the One in control. Jesus spent an abundance of time in prayer with the Father when He was on earth. In order to do the greater works that Jesus spoke about in John, we must also spend an abundance of time in prayer here on earth (John 14:12).

There is God-given, Holy Spirit power when we pray from a righteous position. "The effective prayer of a righteous man can accomplish much" (James 5:16). Remember, "Elijah was a man with a nature like ours" (5:17), and we know his prayers were empowered. The Spirit's power was used to raise Jesus from the dead, and that same resurrection power is available for the clean, or righteous, child of God today, and to clean those He has called.

The battle for souls is a spiritual battle of prayer in the heavenly places, "For our struggle is not against flesh and blood, but against the rulers, against the powers, against the world forces of this darkness, against the spiritual forces of wickedness in the heavenly places" (Ephesians 6:12).

God doesn't send us out to fight this spiritual battle empty-handed but gives us weapons for our warfare. Paul describes these weapons to the Corinthians,

> *For though we walk in the flesh, we do not war according to the flesh, for the weapons of our warfare are not of the flesh, but divinely powerful for the destruction of fortresses. We are destroying speculations and every lofty thing raised up against the knowledge of God, and we are taking every thought captive to the obedience of Christ (2 Corinthians 10:3–5).*

Have you ever been distracted in prayer? Remember this verse and take those distracting thoughts captive. We can be victorious over distractions by focusing on God and His Word in praise to Him. The devil can't stand worship of God and will flee, taking his distractions with him (James 4:7).

We, as God's people, are called, equipped, and given the power to be victorious in the battle in the heavenly places, like a mighty army for the glory of God. We are in the Lord's army and our obedience is God's best weapon in His arsenal.

It is important to appropriate the whole armor of God to pray in the Spirit for all the saints (Ephesians 6:10–18). Praying for one another, for other believers to be bold and courageous is a vital part of keeping our *spiritual military forces* battle-ready.

God wants to give us victory in prayer, however, the church is asleep and not even going into battle. She must be awakened. Remember, Paul says to wake up! "It is already the hour for you to awaken from sleep" (Romans 13:11). Pray for revival in the church and spiritual awakening for those outside.

A DEFEATED FOE

There is a story about a python in an African village. He got into a house and the owner shot the snake with a fatal bullet. However, the snake did not die right away. A python is a very large snake and in his pain and agony he swished his tail furiously breaking windows, destroying furniture, breaking dishes, and generally causing havoc while he was trying to get out of his misery.

The devil is like that snake. He received the fatal blow from Jesus on the Cross and his end is in sight. He is furious, in pain and agony, anticipating his future in the lake of fire (Revelation 20:10). In his defeat he is trying to create as much havoc as he can in the Lord's house and among His saints before his eternal captivity.

We must realize that the devil is a defeated foe and while we are personally no match for him, our God is all-powerful. Praise God that James gives us the secret to victory: "Submit therefore to God. Resist the devil and he will flee from you. Draw near to God and He will draw near to you" (James 4:7–8).

God is sovereign and in His grace, He has chosen to work through you and me, to equip us for the battle of prayer and to make us victorious for His glory. Whether our prayers are in support of God's other fellow workers (see Appendix C), or for those who do not yet know Jesus as Savior (see Appendix B), when we battle in the heavenly places on our knees, we are truly working with God. We are seeking for God's will to be done on earth as it is in heaven.

GET READY TO BE THE ANSWER TO PRAYER

Jesus gave the Great Commission so that we would know what He wants us to do. He said, "Go . . . make disciples . . .

teaching them to observe all that I commanded you" (Matthew 28:19–20). God gives His children spiritual gifts so that believers can be equipped to, "Go . . . make disciples . . . teaching them to observe all that I commanded you." It may sound repetitive, but that's the way multiplication works best. Get very good at the main thing and do it often.

In his high priestly prayer, Jesus said that He "glorified [the Father] on earth, having accomplished the work that [the Father] gave [Him] to do." Then He continued, "As You sent Me into the world, I also have sent them into the world" (John 17:4, 18). To help us understand that He was praying for us today, He said, "I do not ask in behalf of these alone, but for those also who believe in Me through their word" (17:20).

Thankfully, Jesus doesn't leave us to our own devices to accomplish His work. He prayed for us while He was on the earth, and "He always lives to make intercession for [us]" in heaven, at the right hand of the Father (Hebrews 7:25; Romans 8:34). We are not alone in the work of praying for those who don't yet know Jesus, nor are we alone when we have opportunity to share the good news with them.

I like what pastor, author, and missions leader David Platt says about this. "No more spectators in the church. God has not saved you to sideline you. He has saved you to send you out." It makes sense that if our salvation was only to secure our place in heaven God would just *beam us up* when we were saved.

However, He keeps us in the world so that we can be the light of the world to rescue the perishing. I love the old hymn, "Send the Light" by Charles H. Gabriel: "There are souls to rescue, there are souls to save. Send the light! Send the light! Send the light, the blessed gospel light; let it shine from shore to shore."

Think of our mission as disaster relief. We seem to roll up our sleeves and get to work when there is an emergency. People are still in captivity to the devil and that is a big enough disaster for us to let His light shine.

We may work or volunteer in an environment of unbelievers who use foul language and profanity. We have a choice. We can become numb to it or we can ask God to bring His presence to bear on our situation.

After praying and asking for His perspective, we'll more easily see an ungodly situation as a mission field. We can approach it like Jesus did when He spent time with sinners. He quickly went to the heart of the matter, their need of a Savior. We, too, can do that if we stay alert and continually renew our minds with God's Word.

We bring the light of Jesus to our situations because of the indwelling of the Holy Spirit. Dr. Lewis Drummond talked about how the face of Moses glowed when he came off the mountain because of the time he had spent with God (Exodus 34:29–35).

Then he asked the question, "Are we spending so much time with God that our faces glow?" Psalm 34:5 says, "They looked to Him and were radiant, and their faces will never be ashamed."

Our faces may not literally glow, but when we spend much time with God, others can tell there is something different about us. We walk in the joy of the Lord and show compassionate interest in others. Being unashamed of the gospel, too, in a winsome way, will cause co-workers, neighbors, or family members to know our faith in Christ is genuine.

Praying privately for co-workers, neighbors, or family members is the best way to begin to see them as Jesus does, "sheep without a shepherd" (Mark 6:34). Then as we have opportunity, we can offer to pray for them about their felt needs such as an illness, job issue, or family matter.

Our sincerity and followup may very well lead to spiritual conversations. It is important that we spend time with and get to know nonbelievers, but we must remember to boldly bring Jesus with us to give them a chance to meet Him too.

Peter addresses this in his first letter, saying, "But sanctify Christ as Lord in your hearts, always being ready to make a defense to everyone who asks you to give an account for the hope that is in you, yet with gentleness and reverence" (I Peter 3:15). Are we living in such a way and wearing such a radiance or glow that people are coming up to us to ask us to explain why we have hope? Do they see us as people who have been with Jesus? I actually saw this kind of activity one time.

During the 1996 World Olympics in Atlanta, I was blessed to visit all of the prayer venues along with the future prayer chair for Quest Sydney 2000. Glenda was here from Australia to observe what I was doing as current prayer chair, to pray with me, and to participate in the ongoing prayer efforts.

Pray Atlanta '96, as part of Quest Atlanta '96 had been mobilizing prayer for five years, leading up to the outreach events being planned for those precious two weeks when the world would be in our city. Intercessors from other cities across America and in countries around the world were joining us in prayer for God's will to be done.

God heard those prayers and punched holes in the dark clouds over the city to reveal the bright light of the Holy Spirit, who was then unhindered in His work. We witnessed Christian groups working together in a spirit of unity, helping each other with materials in the various languages.

These were groups that normally would not have preferred to work with each other, happily working together on the busy sidewalk. It was amazing. But the most amazing thing was that people on the street were coming up to Christians asking them about Jesus.

Glenda and I went into a restaurant on Peachtree Street to take a break and get a bite to eat. While we were waiting for a table, a man came up to us in great excitement to show us his photograph. He did not speak English and I said, "Oh, you just got married!" seeing the lady beside him (in the photo) dressed in a long, white dress. He understood a little English because he said, "No, Jesus," and he pointed to his heart. We finally understood by his gestures and what was written on the photo folder, that he had just met Jesus. He was excited to tell everyone who would listen.

After lunch, we searched for the group that had three-member teams: a woman dressed in an antebellum dress with a parasol, a photographer, and one who enlisted passersby to have their photo taken with an antebellum lady. While he or she was having his or her photo taken and waiting for it to be developed, the one who enlisted him or her would share the gospel and ask if he or she would like to know Jesus too.

The ministry leaders were thrilled to hear of the man we met and told us how amazed they were that people were ready to receive Christ in record numbers. God working through the fervent prayers of His followers was the secret to that spiritual awakening atmosphere. I want to see that again!

Fast forward to our day and we find that the gospel is not popular now, and we may face persecution for sharing the gospel, but we will not be alone. Jesus reassured the disciples,

> But when they hand you over, do not worry about how or what you are to say; for it will be given you in that hour what you are to say. For it is not you who speak, but it is the Spirit of your Father who speaks in you (Matthew 10:19–20).

The early church was so on fire about Jesus that they didn't pray for protection in the face of persecution; they prayed for boldness to share the gospel. Listen in to the end of their prayer and see its effect as recorded in Acts 4:29–31.

> *And now, Lord, take note of their threats, and grant that Your bond-servants may speak Your word with all confidence, while You extend Your hand to heal, and signs and wonders take place through the name of Your holy servant Jesus. And when they had prayed, the place where they had gathered together was shaken, and they were all filled with the Holy Spirit and began to speak the word of God with boldness.*

God was pleased to answer their kingdom-focused prayer. That is an example of truly working with God in prayer.

My husband, Joel, has a favorite gospel song recorded by the Cathedrals that is entitled, "I've Read the Back of the Book," pointing to the Book of Revelation, (and we win!). Sometimes we look too long at the circumstances around us and not long enough into our Savior's face. I repeat, Jesus defeated Satan on the Cross when He conquered sin and death. We pray from a winning position and need to pray for each other to be bold, strong, and courageous.

God loves to answer "seemingly impossible" prayer requests

because when only He could have done it, He gets the glory without question. The lost are also drawn to Him when they see something they cannot explain. Those mountaintop experiences in our prayer lives also inspire us to remain faithful in the day-to-day *normal* prayertimes.

Pray with Me

Father God,

Thank You for choosing us and equipping us for every good work You give us to do. Keep us aware that we are in a battle in the heavenly places and do not fight flesh and blood. Mighty Warrior, awaken your church out of slumber, revive us so that we may stand firm as Your mighty army empowered by Your Spirit for the sake of Your Name. Give us strength to labor in prayer for those who are being held captive to the deceitfulness of the devil. Draw them to Jesus, we pray, and bring another great spiritual awakening that will usher souls into Your kingdom. Be glorified King Jesus.

In Your name we pray. Amen.

For Further Study

Read Ephesians 6:10–20.

• Name and explain the pieces of the uniform for prayer

• After putting on the armor, what are we told to do?

• Is this battle optional for the Christian?

Read 1 Corinthians 16:13–14.

• What four things are we told to do?

• What does love have to do with the battle?

Read 1 Corinthians 15:57–58.

• List two things about the victory.

• What encouragement is in verse 58?

CONCLUSION
GLORIFYING GOD AND EXPANDING HIS KINGDOM

"That which God abundantly makes the subject of His promises, God's people should abundantly make the subject of their prayers."

—JONATHAN EDWARDS

"On his knees the believer is invincible."

—C. H. SPURGEON

"Be diligent to preserve the unity of the Spirit in the bond of peace. There is one body, and one Spirit, just as also you were called in one hope of your calling; one Lord, one faith, one baptism, one God and Father of all who is over all and through all and in all."

—EPHESIANS 4:3–6

*A*s God's fellow workers, His intercessors, we hold in our hands the key to revival in the church and spiritual awakening across our land. God is awakening and calling His people back to Himself and is working through our prayers of agreement (Matthew 18:19–20). The more we grow in the unity of the Spirit of our Lord and Savior, the more successful we will be in bringing Him the glory He so richly deserves.

When we are united, the devil cannot get through, and that is why he is continually creating conflict within the body of Christ. We must stop falling for His tactics and turning on one another. Division in our ranks gives the devil opportunities for evil, but our love for one another stops him in his tracks!

With all our diversity of ethnic groups, ages, gender, styles of worship, pretribulation and posttribulation ideologies, denominations, parachurch ministries, total immersion baptizers, sprinklers, and more, we can lose sight of the main thing—that Jesus died for our sins, rose again and is victorious! He prayed that we would be one, and He is looking for His holy people.

We can link arms with fellow believers and truly be a mighty force against evil. By remembering the greatness of God, His mighty deeds, His ability, power, and control, we will pray audacious, seemingly impossible prayers. Remember—the gates of hell will not overpower the church (Matthew 16:18). God equips us to be on the offense, under His authority over our defeated foe, the devil, not allowing the devil *any opportunity* against the current church (Ephesians 4:27).

We must rise up and take our stand; our King's name is at stake! We will prevail when we do God's work His way, in His strength, and in His power. Let us be found faithful to consecrate ourselves, to pray without ceasing, both alone in our closets receiving personal orders from our Commander in Chief and very often in agreement with other Christ followers. God has much He wants to do through our prayers if we are willing and persistent.

There is power in praying in agreement. Past revivals have begun when people gathered in obedience to the call of God to pray without ceasing in one accord. A small book written by Jonathan Edwards and published in 1747 has survived and is worth reading. It is now titled *A Call to United Extraordinary Prayer,* published by Christian Heritage, 2003.

God's call, then and again today, is for believers far and wide to unite in earnest prayer to plead with the only One able to bring revival to His people again:

> *Thus says the LORD of hosts, "It will yet be that peoples will come, even the inhabitants of many cities. The inhabitants of one will go to another, saying, 'Let us go at once to entreat the favor of the LORD, and to seek the LORD of hosts; I will also go.' So many peoples and mighty nations will come to seek the LORD of hosts in*

Jerusalem and to entreat the favor of the LORD"
(Zechariah 8:20–22).

Edwards, in reference to these verses, believed that God's rich promises encourage us to expect great success from corporate prayer. He said: "That which God abundantly makes the subject of His promises, God's people should abundantly make the subject of their prayers." He concluded that when believers persevere in united, concerted prayer, God will grant a fresh revival, which "shall be propagated, till the awakening reaches those that are in the highest stations, and till whole nations be awakened."

Let's join with others to entreat the favor of the Lord, with His praise on our lips, marching as to war, both in song and in prayer, moving forward. God inhabits the praise of His people and He is our banner (Psalm 22:3; Exodus 17:15). God establishes a clear link between praise and successful warfare repeatedly in the Old Testament and then referenced by John, in the New Testament:

> *And I saw something like a sea of glass mixed with fire, and those who had been victorious over the beast and his image and the number of his name, standing on the sea of glass, holding harps of God. And they sang the song of Moses, the bond-servant of God, and the song of the Lamb, saying, "Great and marvelous are Your*

works, O Lord God, the Almighty; righteous
and true are Your ways, King of the nations!"
(Revelation 15:2–3).

Pray with me for a mature remnant to arise in our day to be the clean vessels God will choose to use for the extraordinary, united, victorious prayer He longs to answer. May He be pleased to answer our cry for revival in His church and send another great spiritual awakening.

The hymn, "We Are One in the Spirit" is one we could adopt as our theme song to remember how important our unity is to God. There is only one Head and that is Jesus Christ. The rest of us are equal at the foot of the Cross, and each one is vital to the whole body of Christ. To be one in the Spirit, our focus needs to be on the core doctrine of our faith that unites us, not on organization and interpretations that divide. God needs us to be mature Christian soldiers. Read Ephesians 4:1–6, and meditate on these verses as you pray for a mature remnant to arise.

Not only does God honor agreement in prayer, but the encouragement and accountability we gain in praying together is worth seeking out one or two others right where you are, to join in beginning this kind of commitment. Will you be one that God uses to rally the troops in your sphere of influence to pray until spiritual awakening comes?

We can all join with national calls to pray together. Some of the national ministry organizations that offer information for getting involved include the following:

- The National Prayer Committee (nationalprayercommittee .com);
- The National Day of Prayer (nationaldayofprayer.org);
- One Cry (onecry.com);
- Family Research Council (frc.org);
- Presidential Prayer Team (presidentialprayerteam.com);
- Capitol Hill Prayer Partners (chpponline.blogspot.com); and
- Pray Network (praynetwork.com).

Pray with Me

Heavenly Father,

Join our hearts to pray like saints of old who saw You do miraculous things and bring great awakenings. They continued in united prayer seeking Your glory and Your purposes on earth as it is in heaven. Help us to pray like that, with passion for You and undaunted by time and worldly concerns. Lord, make us people of prayer, available to You night and day, like you describe in Isaiah 62:6. Like watchmen on the wall, taking no rest but reminding You of Your promises and giving You no rest until You revive Your people and bring another spiritual awakening in our day. We love You, Lord, and thank You for the privilege of working with You in prayer.

In Jesus' name, amen.

Read Romans 12:9–20.

• List the character traits expected of a follower of Jesus.

• How can this help train our flesh to submit to the Spirit?

Read Colossians 3:12–17.

• Why are we instructed to forgive others?

• What insight can we learn about prayer from these verses?

Read Acts 1:14; Ephesians 6:18; and Colossians 3:1–2; 4:2.

• To what are we told to devote ourselves?

• What does *devote* really mean in prayer?

"I have a theory, and I believe it to be true, that there is not a church, chapel, or mission on earth where you cannot have a revival, provided there is a little nucleus of faithful people who will hold on to God until it comes."

—R. A. TORREY

"God shapes the world by prayer. . . . The prayers of God's saints are the capital stock of Heaven, by which Christ carries on his great work upon earth."

—E. M. BOUNDS

APPENDIX A

SCRIPTURAL SOAP FOR CONFESSION OF SIN

This is like a hotel-size bar of soap and is just a starter for repentance and a cleansed life. Let Jesus wash you as in EPHESIANS 5:25–27: "Just as Christ also loved the church and gave Himself up for her, so that He might sanctify her, having cleansed her by the washing of water with the word, that He might present to Himself the church in all her glory, having no spot or wrinkle or any such thing; but that she should be holy and blameless."

HEBREWS 4:12–13, God's Word is "living and active and sharper than any two-edged sword . . . able to judge the thoughts and intentions of the heart," so it is good to look into Scripture and ask God to bring to our attention any overlooked sins that we need to confess.

THOUGHT LIFE

In MATTHEW 15:19, Jesus says "For out of the heart come evil thoughts, murders, adulteries, fornications, thefts, false witness, slanders."

2 CORINTHIANS 10:5, "We are destroying speculations and every lofty thing raised up against the knowledge of God, and we are taking every thought captive to the obedience of Christ."

ROMANS 12:2, "Do not be conformed to this world, but be transformed by the renewing of your mind."

Are you focusing on God's Word above TV, radio, phone, computer, and other attention-grabbers? Do you think more about work and play than about Christ and expanding His kingdom? Does your life look more like the world or like Christ?

JUDGMENTAL ATTITUDE

MATTHEW 7:1–2, Jesus says, "Do not judge so that you will not be judged, for in the way you judge, you will be judged."

What is Jesus saying to you? How does this apply to your life? Ask God to examine your heart to see if you have a judgmental attitude that you are unaware of, and ask Him to change your heart to please Him.

JEALOUSY AND SELFISH AMBITION

JAMES 3:16 says, "For where jealousy and selfish ambition exist, there is disorder and every evil thing."

Do you want what others have? Are you envious of attention shown to someone else? Do you feel left out? Are you striving to get ahead at all costs? What are your motives for your hard work?

PRIDE—TAKING GOD'S GLORY

ISAIAH 42:8 says, "I am the LORD, that is My name; I will not give My glory to another, nor My praise to graven images."

Are you overly proud of your accomplishments? Do you enjoy having people brag about you and what you have done? Are you impressed with your position? Do you point people to Jesus or try to make yourself look good in their eyes? Ask God to help you obey His command in Matthew 5:16, "Let your light shine before men in such a way that they may see your good works, and glorify your Father who is in heaven."

USE OF YOUR TONGUE—SPEECH

JAMES 3:5, "So also the tongue is a small part of the body, and yet it boasts of great things."

PROVERBS 12:18, "There is one who speaks rashly like the thrusts of a sword, but the tongue of the wise brings healing."

EPHESIANS 4:29, "Let no unwholesome word proceed from your mouth, but only such a word as is good for edification according to the need of the moment, that it may give grace to those who hear."

Does your speech please your heavenly Father? Do you ever use filthy language, tell slightly vulgar jokes, or listen to them? Do you check to make sure what you are saying is true? Do you struggle with gossip? Are you known as an encourager or a nag?

FORGIVENESS

MATTHEW 6:14–15, "For if you forgive others for their transgressions, your heavenly Father will also forgive you. But if you do not forgive others, then your Father will not forgive your transgressions."

Are you harboring a grudge against someone? Do you remember a hurt that seems too hard to forgive? Are you willing with God's help to turn it loose? Ask God to empower you to give it to Him. (See Romans 12:17–21.)

PRAYER AS A LIFESTYLE

1 THESSALONIANS 5:17, "Pray without ceasing."

PSALM 5:3, "In the morning, O LORD, You will hear my voice; in the morning I will order my prayer to You and eagerly watch."

Do you have a regular time to read your Bible and talk with God? How often are you aware of His presence with you in your daily routine? Do you talk to God about everything or only in a crisis?

FORGETFULNESS

PSALM 77:11, "I shall remember the deeds of the LORD; surely I will remember Your wonders of old."

Do you know the biblical wonders that God performed? Are you aware of God's activity all around you today? Do you remember how great God is and talk about Him with others?

SCRIPTURE MEMORY

PSALM 119:11, "Your word I have treasured in my heart, that I may not sin against You."

Are you making an effort to memorize Scripture?

SIN OF OMISSION

JAMES 4:17, "Therefore, to one who knows the right thing to do and does not do it, to him it is sin."

Was there a kindness you could have shown, but you didn't? Are you hoarding the spiritual gifts God has given you to use for edification of the body?

USE OF MONEY

MALACHI 3:8, "Will a man rob God? Yet you are robbing Me! But you say, 'How have we robbed You?' In tithes and offerings."

Do you know that God owns everything and we are His stewards? Does that affect how you use your money? Do you give a tithe of your income to support God's work in your church first?

GOD FORGIVES OUR SINS

PSALM 79:9, "Help us, O God of our salvation, for the glory of Your name; and deliver us, and forgive our sins for Your name's sake."

ISAIAH 43:25, "I, even I, am the one who wipes out your transgressions for My own sake, and I will not remember your sins."

I JOHN 1:9, "If we confess our sins, He is faithful and righteous to forgive us our sins and to cleanse us from all unrighteousness."

APPENDIX B

HOW TO PRAY BIBLICALLY FOR LOST PEOPLE

Understand that the person you are praying for is God's purchased possession—in the name of Jesus and on the basis of His shed blood. "In Him we have redemption through His blood" (Ephesians 1:7).

Ask God to tear down the works of Satan, like false doctrine, unbelief, or other teaching that the enemy may have built up in a person's life. Pray for his thoughts to be taken "captive to the obedience of Christ" (2 Corinthians 10:5).

Pray that the Holy Spirit will convict him of his sin and his need for a Savior. "The kindness of God leads you to repentance" (Romans 2:4).

Pray that the person will hear, receive, or read God's Word and that God's purposes will be accomplished through Scripture. "So will My word be which goes forth from My mouth; it will not return to Me empty, without accomplishing what I desire" (Isaiah 55:11).

Pray that the person's eyes will be opened and ears unstopped so that the truth is heard. "And even if our gospel is veiled, it is veiled to those who are perishing, in whose case the god of this world has blinded the minds of the unbelieving so that they might not see the light of the gospel of the glory of Christ, who is the image of God" (2 Corinthians 4:3-4).

Pray with consistency and perseverance, not to persuade God but because of the resistance of the enemy. Read Daniel 10:12–13. "Therefore, my beloved brethren, be steadfast, immovable, always abounding in the work of the Lord, knowing that your toil is not in vain in the Lord" (1 Corinthians 15:58).

Thank God for making us more than conquerors. "But in all these things we overwhelmingly conquer through Him who loved us" (Romans 8:37). "Thanks be to God, who gives us the victory through our Lord Jesus Christ" (1 Corinthians 15:57).

The key is for the lost person's heart to be changed by the saving power of Christ. Use the acrostic HEART to jog your memory. Pray for him or her to have:
• A receptive HEART (see Luke 8:5, 12).
• EYES to be open (see Matthew 13:15; 2 Corinthians 4:3–4).
• God's ATTITUDE toward sin (see John 16:8).
• RELEASE to believe (see 2 Timothy 2:25–26).
• A TRANSFORMED life (see Romans 12:1–2).

Ask God for an opportunity to invite this person to a harvest event. "Go out into the highways and along the hedges, and compel them to come in, so that my house may be filled" (Luke 14:23).

Appendix B adapted from If My People . . . Pray *by Elaine Helms.*

APPENDIX C

SAMPLE PRAYER FOR ANOTHER BELIEVER

This is a sample biblical prayer we can pray for a fellow Christian going through spiritual warfare:

Father,

I lift up (name) to You and thank You, Lord, that you have covered [him or her] with the blood of Jesus and the devil can only roar as he prowls around causing trouble. Father, thank You for giving us Your protection from evil. I pray that (name) will be dressed in "the full armor of God so that [he or she] will be able to stand firm against the schemes of the devil. For our struggle is not against flesh and blood" (Ephesians 6:11–12). I am so thankful that You tell us "[We] are from God . . . and have overcome them; because greater is He who is in [us] than he who is in the world" (1 John 4:4).

Lord, give (name) Your victory in this spiritual battle and may [his or her] faith grow even stronger because of seeing You show Yourself strong on [his or her] behalf, as You promise in 2 Chronicles 16:9. You are mighty to save, Lord, and You are giving charge to Your angels to guard (name) right now. We praise You using Psalm 91, and thank You that "he who dwells in the shelter of the Most High will abide in the shadow of the Almighty." (Name) can say to You, Lord, "my refuge and my fortress, my God in whom I trust!"

Father, I ask that (name) will be anxious for nothing, but in everything through prayer and petition with thanksgiving make his requests known to You, so that you can flood [him or her] with Your peace that passes all understanding (Philippians 4:6–7). Lord God, this battle is Yours because You tell us in Zechariah 4:6, it will be won "not by might, nor by power, but by [Your] Spirit." Hallelujah! All glory to You, God Almighty. You are the Victor.

In Jesus' name, amen.

New Hope® Publishers is a division of WMU®, an international organization that challenges Christian believers to understand and be radically involved in God's mission. For more information about WMU, go to wmu.com. More information about New Hope books may be found at NewHopeDigital.com. New Hope books may be purchased at your local bookstore.

Use the QR reader on your
smartphone to visit us online at
NewHopeDigital.com

If you've been blessed by this book, we would like to hear your story.
The publisher and author welcome your comments and
suggestions at: newhopereader@wmu.org.